Horace Bushnell on Women in Nineteenth-Century America

Michiyo Morita

University Press of America,® Inc.
Dallas · Lanham · Boulder · New York · Oxford

4501 Forbes Boulevard
Suite 200
Lanham, Maryland 20706
UPA Acquisitions Department (301) 459-3366

PO Box 317
Oxford
OX2 9RU, UK

Printed in the United States of America
British Library Cataloging in Publication Information Available

Library of Congress Control Number: 2004106839
ISBN 0-7618-2888-5 (paperback : alk. ppr.)

™ The paper used in this publication meets the minimum requirements of American National Standard for Information Sciences—Permanence of Paper for Printed Library Materials, ANSI Z39.48—1984

CONTENTS

ACKNOWLEDGMENTS

I would like to offer a prayer of my gratitude to God. Without God's help, I could not have completed this book. During the past four years, I have felt God's special care for me.

Many people helped me with this project. First of all, I want to express my thanks from the bottom of my heart to Dr. and Chair of Seigakuin board of trustees, Hideo Ohki. He gave me time and a place (General Research Institute of Seigakuin University) to finish this book without financial problems. I also appreciate the continual encouragement of Dr. Yasuo Furuya who is Professor of the Graduate School of Seigakuin University.

Without Dr. Janet Stafford, my academic friend for over ten years, I could not have done with this work. My heartfelt appreciation is extended to her. She always walked with me in the journey toward the accomplishment of this project.

Dr. Yasuko Grosjean read my draft of this book in early stage, and gave valuable comments. Dr. Paula Cameron also read my manuscript in the final stage, and provided important suggestions and comments. I greatly appreciate their help.

This book is based on my dissertation submitted to the Caspersen School of Graduate Studies of Drew University for the degree, Doctor of Philosophy. I heartily address my gratitude to the dissertation committee members: Professors Kenneth E. Rowe, Donald W. Dayton, and Jesse T. Todd. They were instrumental in teaching me the rigor and enjoyment of scholarship. Professor Rowe sent all of his Bushnell materials from America to me in Japan upon his retirement. I am very proud of that. Janet F. Fishburn, Professor Emeritus of Drew University, was interested in my topic and encouraged me. Professor Katherine G. Brown greatly helped me during my time in residence at Drew.

I am also grateful to University Press of America which made it possible for this book to be published. Furthermore, I thank anonymous readers for reviewing my manuscript.

Lastly, I would like to express my devout thanks to Mr. Shiro Matsuo, my brother-in law, and Mrs. Emiko Morita and Mrs. Fujie Matsuo, my two sisters. Without their loving support, I could not have finished this book.

May God bless this book, and allow it to be used for further improvement of Horace Bushnell scholarship in the world!

CHAPTER 1
INTRODUCTION

The Thesis of This Book

Horace Bushnell (1802-1876) is well known as a precursor of liberalism in American Protestant Christian theology. He also is renowned as a father of American Christian education, as a notable pastor and preacher, and as a commentator on the American social and political situation of his time. In addition, he is considered a minister who contributed to the so-called "feminization" of nineteenth-century American religion.[1]

However, when one focuses on Bushnell's views of women in terms of family, church and nation in nineteenth-century America, he emerges as a different man from the figure investigated by other scholars. He envisioned a Christian America[2] based on the organic unity of family, church, and nation. A Christian America was not a reality, but a goal for Bushnell and other nineteenth-century American Christians. Bushnell presumed a "Christian America" would be a nation that endorsed basic Christian beliefs. Furthermore, he was confident that the Christian religion would take the lead in shaping American culture.

Bushnell believed that the institutions of family, church, and nation were organic, and were the cornerstones in forming, maintaining, and expanding a Christian America. Although he frequently used the term "organic," Bushnell did not offer a clear definition of the word. Allen C. Guelzo suggests that Bushnell used "organic" to indicate "a sense of wholeness or connectedness."[3]

He hoped to encourage the formation of a Christian America by emphasizing the importance of men's "government" of women and women's "subordination" to men. This means that men, by nature, should have the "governmental" function, while women should carry the "subordinate" function.[4] His views on women, therefore, were generally patriarchal and hierarchical. However, in certain situations his attitudes toward women were egalitarian and nurturing. Consequently, his understandings of women were not simplistic, but displayed complexity.

Therefore, to fully understand Bushnell and his significance as a nineteenth-century American Christian man, it is important to engage in a systematic study of his views on women in the settings of family, church, and nation. These comprise the foundations of his vision for a Christian America.

Profound Changes in the First Half of the Nineteenth Century

Horace Bushnell was born on April 14, 1802, in Litchfield, Connecticut, at the beginning of a century of profound change. Early nineteenth-century American society had been an agricultural, communal society. At the time of Bushnell's birth, most of people lived on farms, enjoying a slow-paced life.[5] However, the next sixty years saw a shift from an agrarian, communal society to an industrial, individualistic society. Factories and railroads were built to produce and move goods across the country. With these changes came a shift in family economics. Men, older children, and single women moved from home-based employment to the factory in search of wages. This brought a new, increasingly urban world that seemed to be individualistic and constantly on the move. Meanwhile, in accord with earlier expectations, married women were supposed to raise the children and oversee the operation of the household. In addition, religious and educational leaders told mothers that they had a profound impact on their children and that proper child-rearing was essential to the fate of the nation.[6]

Around the turn of the nineteenth century, the great wave of revivals, known as the Second Great Awakening, spread across the country for about two generations.[7] Winthrop S. Hudson and John Corrigan note that women made up the majority of revival converts.[8] Through participation in the revivals, women converts experienced a degree of liberty from the restrictions of male control, acquired self-confidence and discovered an independent way of living. Also, women began to learn the organizational skills necessary to form groups and societies, and gained an awareness of the importance of mission.[9] Catherine Clinton observes that women reacted passionately to the Second Great Awakening. She writes that females "were widely lauded for their 'special' ability to spread religion, particularly to children."[10]

The first half of the nineteenth century also saw the emergence of the first wave of feminism in America. Through their involvement in social activities and movements, women (middle-class women in particular) came to realize that they were being denied equality simply on the basis of their sex. In 1848, the Seneca Falls Convention formally called for a change in the treatment of women. Leading suffragists such as Elizabeth Cady Stanton, Susan B. Anthony, Mary Ann McClintock and others sought to mobilize American women to fight for their rights and, most radically of all, to fight for the right to vote.

In the midst of these changes, came another shift. In 1818, the establishment between church and state ended in Connecticut. By 1833, the same year that Bushnell entered the ministry, Massachusetts became the last state in America to forbid a church-state connection. The change resulted in a loss of community power for previously established churches, such as New England's Congregational churches, because they were forced to compete with other denominations for parishioners and funds.[11]

Thus, Bushnell lived in an era of profound changes: the emergence of an industrial and individualistic society, revivalism, women's suffrage, and disestablishment. His life was a response to these changes.

Bushnell's Brief Life History until His Marriage

Bushnell's parents were Ensign Bushnell and Dotha Bishop Bushnell. They were farming people. His father was a Methodist of the Arminian type, while his mother was an Episcopalian. The only church in Litchfield at that time was Episcopalian; the couple baptized their son Horace there. But, after moving a few miles away from Litchfield to New Preston, Bushnell's parents became members of the "Calvinistic Congregational" church.[12] In 1821, at the age of nineteen, Bushnell also joined that congregation.

After graduation from Yale Divinity School in 1832, Bushnell met and fell in love with Mary Mehitable Apthorp. At the time, Apthorp was living in New Haven with her mother and sisters. She was a descendant, on her mother's side, of John Davenport, the first minister of New Haven. Bushnell had been teaching a Bible class made up of young women at the Third Congregational Church of New Haven when he first encountered the bright, attractive, twenty-seven-year-old.[13] Their courtship was swift. Bushnell began his ministry in February 1833, and a few months later, on September 13, he and Mary Apthorp were married.[14]

Bushnell's Own Family

Bushnell and his wife had four daughters and one son. Their first daughter, Frances Louisa (1834-1899), rarely was in good health. Despite this, as an adult she became a member of the teaching staff at the Hartford Public High School.[15] Elizabeth Davenport was born in 1836 and died in 1837. In 1838, their only son, Horace Apthorp, was born, but the child died in 1842. Mary Bushnell (1840-1917) was their fourth child. She joined the North Congregational Church when she was ten years old. Prior to marriage, Mary Bushnell taught at Sarah Porter's fashionable finishing academy in Farmington.[16] After her marriage to Frank W. Cheney in 1863, she became the mother of twelve children and wrote her father's biography.[17] The Bushnell's youngest daughter, Dotha (1843-1932), was married in her mid-thirties.[18] In 1930 Dotha was given an honorary M.A. from Trinity College in Hartford.[19]

Hartford

The Bushnells made their home in Hartford, Connecticut where Horace Bushnell served as pastor of the North Congregational Church from 1833 until 1859. In the 1830s, Hartford was in a major economic transition from ocean-going commerce to nationally recognized banking, insurance, publishing, manufacturing, and merchandising enterprises.[20] The railroad came to Hartford in 1839, and this event had a strong impact on the city's industry and society.[21] As a result of these changes, Hartford's population grew rapidly. With 6,901 inhabitants in 1820, the figure expanded to 9,787 by 1830, to 12,793 by 1840, to 13,552 by 1850, and to 29,152 by 1860.[22]

In the 1830's, as Bushnell was just beginning his ministry, Hartford had twelve houses of worship. According to J. Eugene Smith, the city possessed five Congregationalist, two Baptist, one Episcopalian, one Methodist, one Universalist, one Roman Catholic, and one "African" congregation.[23]

Bushnell's Congregation: The North Congregational Church

When Bushnell began his pastorate at the North Congregational Church, there were 264 members. By 1842, there were 447. By the time Bushnell resigned from the Church in 1859, the total number was 490.[24]

Bushnell's parishioners were urbanized, middle-class New Englanders, politically conservative and religiously earnest.[25] His congregation especially represented the mercantile class, and was comprised of manufacturers, bankers, commission merchants, insurance executives, retailers, shopkeepers, and artisans.[26] In addition, the North Congregational Church included professional men such as teachers and lawyers, a handful of ordained ministers, and a few ministerial wives and widows.[27]

Among the parishioners was John P. Brace, head of the Hartford Female Seminary, which was founded by Catharine Beecher in 1823.[28] Another member was lawyer Thomas C. Perkins, the husband of Mary Beecher, one of Lyman Beecher's daughters. The congregation also included Samuel Porter, a pioneer teacher at the American School for the Deaf.[29]

As children, Charles H. Clark and Charles L. Brace attended Bushnell's North Congregational Church. Clark later became an editor at the Hartford *Courant*, and Brace was a founder of the Children's Aid Society in New York City. Another parishioner was Aaron L. Chapin, who later served as president of Beloit College. Thomas K. Beecher, a son of Lyman Beecher, also attended Bushnell's church and became a minister at the Park Congregational Church of Elmira, New York. Frederick L. Olmsted, architect and later designer of New York's Central Park, was also a member of Bushnell's congregation; as was Henry C. Trumbull, who became an influential leader in American Christian education.[30] Clearly, Bushnell's congregation contained numerous people in the business and professional classes of Hartford, many of whom played a prominent role in nineteenth-century American society and culture.

History of Research

Scholars have investigated Bushnell from many angles. Within their scholarship, the following themes have emerged: theology, education, social and political thought, and women's issues. Robert L. Edwards, for instance, reviewed Bushnell's life and work in order to illuminate the many aspects of his life: pastor and preacher of the North Congregational Church in Hartford, presenter of a Copernican idea of "nurture" in Christian education, commentator on the social, cultural and political condition of his time, and theologian.[31] Another set of themes are provided by Robert Bruce Mullin, who regarded Bushnell as both a Yankee and a Puritan: an innovator and a conservative.[32]

Conrad Cherry analyzes the characteristic notions of nature and imagination in terms of Bushnell's religious symbolism.[33] Cherry believes that Bushnell's notion of nature lacked flexibility and was, in fact, rigid.[34] David L. Smith has studied Bushnell's theory of communication.[35] According to Smith, Bushnell understood that the forms of God's self-revelation—Christ, nature, Scripture, and theological formulas—should all serve as vehicles for the communication of a divine character to humankind.[36] James O. Duke treats Bushnell as one who tried to "overcome dogmatism without falling prey to historicism."[37]

Randolph Crump Miller,[38] Sara Little,[39] and Jerry W. McCant studied Bushnell's philosophy of Christian education and its advocacy of the nurture of children within Christian values. According to McCant, Bushnell did not rely on a completely maternal model of nurture.[40] McCant's argument is relevant to my study, because, in my view, Bushnell's nurturing model was paternalistic as well as maternalistic. In other words, Bushnell depended on both "father-centered and mother-centered" models of nurture.

Many have studied Horace Bushnell as a commentator on social and political issues of his era. For instance, Conrad Cherry had analyzed Bushnell's notion of organic thinking.[41] Cherry writes that Bushnell understood America to be "a nation organically covenanted with God, one nation united under God's sovereignty."[42] His analysis is helpful in understanding that Bushnell's desire for a Christian America was based upon the organic unity of family, church, and nation.

Howard A. Barnes contrasts two social and political theories—Bushnell's organic theory and Jefferson's social contract theory—both of which are critical to an understanding of Bushnell's views on nation.[43] Bushnell understood that a nation should be organic and united with God. He opposed Jefferson's social contract theory because it was strongly human-centered and lacked the participation of God in social and political structures.

Daniel Walker Howe regards Bushnell as "typical of American conservatives." Howe is also the first scholar to point out the lack of a careful, scholarly analysis of Bushnell's idea of women's rights, even though this aspect of Bushnell's thought was not Howe's main concern.[44]

Thus, most scholars have neglected to investigate Bushnell's views on women's issues. However, both "Femininity and the Nineteenth Century Post-Puritan Mind," a dissertation by Ronald William Hogeland,[45] and *The Feminization of American Culture*, a notable yet controversial study by Ann Douglas, do discuss certain aspects of Bushnell's attitudes toward women. Hogeland argues that Bushnell manifested a masculine ambivalence toward femininity.[46] I, however, believe that Bushnell did not have ambivalent attitudes toward women. Rather, I have come to understand that his attitudes were complex. Although in most cases he held patriarchal and hierarchical views, there were some circumstances in which his attitudes were egalitarian and nurturing.[47] In addition, Hogeland does not analyze Bushnell's views on women in terms of the nation. This is an important area of investigation that should not be neglected, since Bushnell strongly rejected female participation in the politics of the nation.

Douglas contends that the endorsement of "feminization" in nineteenth-century New England simultaneously guaranteed the continuation of American "male hegemony."[48] She singles out and criticizes Bushnell for his attitudes toward women, and for his endorsement of "male hegemony."[49] Although I agree with Douglas's argument that Bushnell endorsed "male hegemony," I disagree with her when she contends that "the women addressed by Bushnell . . . were both flattered and threatened."[50] My research indicates that the women addressed by him, including members of his own family, were neither flattered nor threatened by his discourse.

On the other hand, in recent years, historical studies of women's issues—such as women's roles, spheres, and rights—have grown and expanded considerably. The following scholarship offers perspectives of Bushnell's views on women that are different from those presented by Hogeland and Douglas.

Nancy F. Cott provides useful categories for analysis of the natures of men and women through two specific models: the hierarchy model and the contrast model.[51] Cott notes that one ought to pay particular attention to whether the ideological differentiation of men and women rested principally on hierarchy or on contrast.[52] Cott then introduces Thomas Laqueur's work, and comments:

> Laqueur identifies a shift by the mid-eighteenth century from traditional use of the same criteria for assessing male and female characteristics—a standard by which the female is usually found inferior—to the use of standards

> of what he [Laqueur] calls incommensurability, in which the two sexes are seen to be so dissimilar that they cannot be measured by the same criteria.[53]

Cott concludes that the shift from the comparable/hierarchical model to the incommensurable model was ambiguous with regard to any actual improvement of women's status, because the theory of incommensurability between men and women clearly was not without hierarchical implications.[54] These two categories help to clarify Bushnell's complex views on the natures of women and men. In most cases, Bushnell viewed the natures of men and women as hierarchical. Yet, there were other cases in which he considered them to be incommensurable.

Linda K. Kerber observes that in the mid-1960s historians such as Barbara Welter, Aileen S. Kraditor, and Gerda Lerner used the metaphor of separate spheres to investigate women's issues in nineteenth-century America.[55] David G. Hackett comments that the ideology of separate spheres in nineteenth-century America meant that men occupied a public sphere, while women were influential in a private sphere.[56] This paradigm, however, does not fully explain Bushnell's views of female and male spheres, because Bushnell did not perceive the spheres of women and men as rigid or fixed. Instead, he had a more fluid understanding of the places occupied by women and men.

Hackett asserts that the separation of the home from the workplace in nineteenth-century America resulted in the removal of men from the home and that the home became women's sphere.[57] But once again this does not help us understand Bushnell's idea of the spheres and roles assigned to each sex, because he did not see the home as completely woman's sphere and work as completely man's sphere. On the other hand, Mary P. Ryan points out that the fundamental structure of the nineteenth-century family was actually a weaving of heterosexual and heterosocial relationships.[58] In a similar vein, Cott adds that male influence actually was not absent from the home in nineteenth-century America.[59] Both Ryan and Cott, therefore, prove to be more useful when analyzing Bushnell's views of each sex's roles and spheres.

Colleen McDannell provides two models of government, education, and worship in the nineteenth-century American family: the paternal model and the maternal model.[60] This categorization also serves as a tool to assess Bushnell's views of the roles of men and women regarding Christian nurture, government and worship in families, because Bushnell did not neglect paternal participation in Christian nurture.

Barbara Welter addresses four cardinal virtues of "True Womanhood": piety, purity, submissiveness and domesticity.[61] As will be discussed later in Chapter 2, Welter's attributes of "True Womanhood" also function as tools for my analysis and interpretation of Bushnell's views on women's issues in the context of the nineteenth-century American family. Paula Baker points out that one of the ironies of Jacksonian democracy was the simultaneous development of the cult of true womanhood.[62] Cott, on the other hand, prefers the term "the cult of domesticity" to the "the cult of true womanhood," because she believes that "it [the cult of domesticity] went beyond insular consideration of women's roles to include all family members."[63] However, I prefer to use the concept of "home" to understand Bushnell's views of women's issues, because he used the term "home" in his writings rather than "domesticity." Additionally, the importance of nurturing children into Christian maturity was one of the most crucial ideas in Bushnell's thinking, and the act of nurturing is better served by Bushnell's concept of "home," rather than "domesticity."[64]

Scholarship on American manhood emerged in the 1990s. One of the scholars, E. Anthony Rotundo, has divided manhood in American history into three general transformational phases: communal manhood, self-made manhood, and passionate manhood.[65] This interpretive scheme for understanding manhood in American social and cultural history is helpful in comprehending Bushnell's views of men, especially men's roles in the family.[66] His views of men's roles in the family, found in *Christian Nurture,* fit the "communal manhood" rather than "self-made manhood" and "passionate manhood" classifications.

Susan Hill Lindley provides three models of women's ministry in nineteenth-century America: the preaching model, the ordination model, and the deaconess model.[67] These models have proved useful in understanding Bushnell's views on women's ministry in the church. They illustrate how Bushnell endorsed the preaching and deaconess models, but not the ordination model. Also useful is Barbara Brown Zikmund's analysis of the basic arguments for and against women preaching in nineteenth-century America,[68] and Jeannine E. Olson's concept that the roles of deacons and deaconesses could be understood within the categories of liturgy and charity.[69] Both of these scholars' ideas provide rationales for Bushnell's support of female preachers and the deaconess movement.

In addition, Leonard I. Sweet offers four models of American ministers' wives from the seventeenth century to the nineteenth century: the Companion model, the Sacrificer model, the Assistant model, and the Partner model.[70] These models give us a structure by which we can comprehend Bushnell's ideas about the general function of ministers' wives and the actual function of his own wife, Mary Apthorp Bushnell. Also helpful were Lois A. Boyd's comments that Presbyterian ministers' wives began to transcend the rigidity of women's sphere,[71] and Julie Roy Jeffrey's contention that some Methodist ministers' wives in the frontier invaded the ministers' sphere.[72] Boyd and Jeffrey provide a key to understanding whether or not Mary Bushnell, as a minister's wife, trespassed on her husband's ministerial sphere.

In the late 1970s and early 1980s, women scholars of American history and gender studies began to discuss differences in the terminology of the women's suffrage movement, the women's rights movement, and the women's emancipation movement in America. Ellen Carol DuBois suggests that for "both opponents and advocates of women's rights, the demand for woman suffrage was significantly more controversial than other demands for equality with men."[73] Thus, the women's suffrage movement and the women's rights movement were overlapping, but not identical movements. DuBois suggests that one should distinguish between the two. The distinction between women's suffrage and women's rights, as well as the women's suffrage movement and the women's emancipation movement is helpful in understanding why Bushnell had different opinions of various women's issues and movements.

Steven M. Buechler provides three ideological traditions of the women's suffrage movement in nineteenth-century America. The first tradition was evangelical Christianity. The second and the third ideological traditions were Enlightenment and socialist feminism respectively.[74] These three views are useful in clarifying the ideological tradition on which Bushnell focused to develop his own views of the women's suffrage movement.

Ellen Carol DuBois deals with the women's suffrage movement on the national level,[75] while Carole Nichol addresses the dynamics of the suffrage movement in Connecticut.[76] To understand the women's suffrage movement on both the national and local levels is useful for comprehending the dynamic process of the movement. Susan E. Marshall points out that Bushnell provided one of the bases for the initial resistance to the women's suffrage movement.[77]

Methodology of This Book

The methodology of this book is the historical analysis and interpretation of primary texts selected from the corpus of Bushnell's writings. One of the key texts that I will use throughout this study is *Women's Suffrage; The Reform Against Nature*, written by Bushnell in 1869.[78] This text is Bushnell's reaction to the women's suffrage movement in nineteenth-century America. Another important text throughout this study is Bushnell's book, *Christian Nurture*, a collection of discourses and essays written from 1847 to 1861.[79] This text, written for Christian parents, emphasizes the importance of nurturing children into Christian maturity within the context of the family. The family, according to Bushnell, was a primary institution for building a Christian America.[80] Finally, as tools of analysis and interpretation of Bushnell's views of women's issues, I make use of the many historical studies, as stated in the previous section.

Outline of This Book

In the next chapter, "Women in the Family," I provide evidence illustrating that Bushnell tried to promote a solid marriage and family life as the ideal, and that he believed this ideal could be accomplished by reinforcing men's patriarchal and hierarchical attitudes toward women. In this way, he hoped to build a secure family as the cornerstone for a Christian America. However, in his own marriage and family life, Bushnell did not realize (nor did he even attempt to realize) his ideal. Due to his poor health, he was often away from home in hope of finding more favorable climatic conditions. Thus, he left many important matters of family life to his wife. His views of woman in marriage and family life, therefore, showed a disjuncture between the ideal and the actual.

In Chapter 3, "Women in the Church," I demonstrate that Bushnell entrusted the building of a strong church foundation not to men, but to women. By making use of women—especially women's religious nature, preaching, deaconess work, and the participation of the pastor's wife in ministry—Bushnell hoped to form solid churches that in turn would build a strong Christian America. His desire was to transform America into a "Christian America." He believed, however, that this transformation would not happen through politics (as the female suffragists believed), but through Christianity via women's activities in the church. Bushnell had confidence in the religious power of women. Yet he rejected women's administration because he thought that it would threaten the patriarchal and hierarchical order of men and women in the church. He also believed that a disruption of church order would eventually destroy the hierarchical, patriarchal order within the larger world of a Christian America. Thus, Bushnell's complexity regarding his views of women was extended to the church.

In Chapter 4, "Women in the Nation," I assert that Bushnell was afraid that women's participation in politics through suffrage would have a negative impact on the foundations of the family, the church and the nation, and that it would lead to the eventual decline of a Christian America based on the organic unity of family, church and nation. However, with the exception of the political arena, Bushnell also believed that women's sphere could be and should be expanded in society. In this sense, his views on women had an egalitarian tendency, as long as women did not involve themselves in politics. Hence, he possessed complex views toward women in terms of their participation in society.

Notes

1 Barbara Welter coined the term, "feminization." However, it was Ann Douglas who applied the word to Horace Bushnell. Barbara Welter, "The Feminization of American Religion: 1800-1860," in *Dimity Convictions: The American Woman in the Nineteenth Century* (Athens: Ohio University Press, 1976). Ann Douglas, *The Feminization of American Culture* (New York: Doubleday, 1977).

Scholars have defined the term "feminization" in various ways. The "feminization" discussions by scholars and my position on them will be described later in this chapter.

2 Robert T. Handy coined the term, "a Christian America." Robert T. Handy, *A Christian America: Protestant Hopes and Historical Realities* (New York: Oxford University Press, 1984), ix-xii. In addition, Handy points out that evangelical Protestantism began to Christianize America about 1815. Robert T. Handy, "Sunday School Movement," in *The Westminster Dictionary of Christian Education*, 1963.

3 Allen C. Guelzo, "Foreword," in *The Puritan as Yankee: A Life of Horace Bushnell* (Grand Rapids: William B. Eerdmans Publishing Company, 2002), xii. A further, detailed discussion of Bushnell's concept of a Christian America based on the organic unity of family, church, and nation can be found in Chapter 4, "Women in the Nation."

4 Regarding men's "governing nature" and women's "subordinate nature," see "Natures of Women and Men" in Chapter 2, which contains a detailed discussion on the subject.

5 Robert L. Edwards, *Of Singular Genius, Of Singular Grace: A Biography of Horace Bushnell* (Cleveland: The Pilgrim Press, 1992), 7-8.

6 Nancy F. Cott, *The Bonds of Womanhood: "Woman's Sphere" in the New England, 1780-1835* (New Haven and London: Yale University Press, 1977), 46.

7 Winthrop S. Hudson and John Corrigan, *Religion in America*, 5th ed. (New York: Macmillan Publishing Company, 1992), 134.

8 Ibid., 141.

9 Ibid., 142.

10 Catherine Clinton, *The Other Civil War: American Women in the Nineteenth Century* (New York: Hill and Wang, 1984), 11.

11 Edwards, *Of Singular Genius, Of Singular Grace*, 108.

12 Horace Bushnell, "Sketches of His Grandmother and Mother," in *Life and Letters of Horace Bushnell*, ed. Mary Bushnell Cheney (New York: Harper & Brothers, Publishers, 1880; reprint, New York: Arno Press & *The New York Times*, 1969), 28. This was written in 1874 at the request of friends.

13 Edwards, *Of Singular Genius, Of Singular Grace*, 38.

14 Mary Bushnell Cheney, ed., *Life and Letters of Horace Bushnell* (New York: Harper & Brothers, Publishers, 1880; reprint, New York: Arno Press & *The New York Times*, 1969), 72.

15 Edwards, *Of Singular Genius, Of Singular Grace*, 217. According to Robert L. Edwards, the Hartford Public High School was established in 1847 by Horace Bushnell with the help of his friend, Henry Barnard. This school was created in part from the Hopkins Grammar School. Ibid., 62.

16 Ibid., 217.

17 Ibid., 241, 291.

18 The exact year is not clear.

19 Edwards, *Of Singular Genius, Of Singular Grace*, 217.

20 Ibid., 41.

21 Glenn Weaver, *Hartford: An Illustrated History of Connecticut's Capital* (Woodland: Windsor Publications, Inc., 1982), 76.

22 Weaver., 78.

23 J. Eugene Smith, *One Hundred Years of Hartford's Courant: From Colonial Times through the Civil War* (New Haven: Yale University Press, 1949), 234.

24 Robert L. Edwards, "Portrait of a People: Horace Bushnell's Hartford Congregation," in *Studies of the Church in History*, ed. Horton Davies (Allison Park: Pickwick Publications, 1983), 150-51.

25 Edwards, *Of Singular Genius, Of Singular Grace*, 138. See also Edwards, "Portrait of a People: Horace Bushnell's Hartford Congregation," 157.

26 Ibid., 153. See also Edwards, *Of Singular Genius, Of Singular Grace*, 2.

27 Edwards, "Portrait of a People: Horace Bushnell's Hartford Congregation," 153-54.

28 Milton Rugoff notes, "It [The Hartford Female Seminary] ranked with Emma Willard's school in Troy, New York, and Zilpah P. Grant's in Ipswich, Massachusetts, as one of the outstanding academies for girls in the United States." Milton Rugoff, *The Beechers: An American Family in the Nineteenth Century* (New York: Harper & Row, Publishers, 1981), 53. Robert L. Edwards notes that although not during Catharine Beecher's administration, Bushnell served for many years as a trustee of the Hartford Female Seminary. Edwards, *Of Singular Genius, Of Singular Grace*, 146.

29 Edwards, "Portrait of a People: Horace Bushnell's Hartford Congregation," 153.

30 Ibid., 155-56.

31 Edwards, *Of Singular Genius, Of Singular Grace*.

32 Robert Bruce Mullin, *The Puritan as Yankee: A Life of Horace Bushnell* (Grand Rapids: William B. Eerdmans Publishing Company, 2002).

33 Conrad Cherry, *Nature and the Religious Imagination: From Edwards to Bushnell* (Philadelphia: Fortress, 1980).

34 Ibid., 203.

35 David L. Smith, *Symbolism and Growth: The Religious Thought of Horace Bushnell* (Chico: Scholars Press, 1981).

36 Smith, *Symbolism and Growth*, xiv.

37 James O. Duke, *Horace Bushnell: On the Vitality of Biblical Language* (Chico: Scholars Press, 1984), 11.

38 Randolph Crump Miller, *Christian Nurture and the Church* (New York: Charles Scribner's Sons, 1961); and "Horace Bushnell: Prophet to America's Children," *Perkins Journal* 32 (1979): 1-8.

39 Sara Little, "Christian Nurture," *American Presbyterians* 66 (Winter 1988): 245-50.

40 Jerry W. McCant, "Nurture Is Not the Problem," *Christian Education Journal* 5, no. 2 (1984): 57-68.

41 Conrad Cherry, "The Structure of Organic Thinking: Horace Bushnell's Approach to Language, Nature, and Nation," *Journal of the American Academy of Religion* 40 (1972): 3-20.

42 Ibid., 13.

43 Howard A. Barnes, "The Idea That Caused a War: Horace Bushnell Versus Thomas Jefferson," *Journal of Church and State* 16, no. 1 (Winter 1974): 73-83; and *Horace Bushnell and the Virtuous Republic* (Metuchen: The Scarecrow Press, Inc., 1991).

44 Daniel Walker Howe, "The Social Science of Horace Bushnell," *The Journal of American History* 70, no. 2 (September 1983): 305-22. *Making the American Self: Jonathan Edwards to Abraham Lincoln* (Cambridge: Harvard University Press, 1997), 175-85. Among Bushnell's contemporaries, Thomas M. Clark, Bushnell's friend and Bishop of Rhode Island, categorized Bushnell as a conservative. Cheney, ed., 296.

45 Ronald William Hogeland, "Femininity and the Nineteenth Century Post-Puritan Mind" (Ph.D. diss., University of California, Los Angeles, 1968).

46 Hogeland, 180.

47 See the exposition of this complexity in the following chapters on Women in the Family, Women in the Church, and Women in the Nation.

48 Douglas, 13.

49 Douglas has been criticized by such scholars as David Schuyler, David S. Reynolds, Ann Taves and Ann Braude. Schuyler notes, "Douglas's assertion that in the aftermath of disestablishment the ministry was forced to cultivate an alliance with women is at best unverified." My reading of Bushnell supports Schuyler's position. David Schuyler, "Inventing a Feminine Past," *The New England Qvarterly* 51 (September 1978): 298.

Reynolds remarks, "To generalize that nineteenth-century American religion became feminized—i.e., more yielding, effeminate—is to overlook the fact that during this period a fervent muscular Christianity began to take shape." According to my reading of Bushnell, I understand that he favored "a muscular Christianity" for a strong Christian America. David S. Reynolds, "The Feminization Controversy: Sexual Stereotypes and the Paradoxes of Piety in Nineteenth-century America," *The New Englander Quarterly* 53 (1980): 99.

Ann Taves writes, "The changes Douglas describes as 'feminizing' were not necessarily perceived in that way by mid-nineteenth-century Christians." Ann Taves, "Mothers and Children and the Legacy of Mid-nineteenth-Century American Christianity," *Journal of Religion* 67, no. 2 (1987): 203. In addition, Ann Braude argues, "Female majorities were nothing new in the nineteenth century." Ann Braude, "Women's History Is American Religious History," in *Retelling U.S. Religious History*, ed. Thomas A. Tweed (Berkeley: University of California Press, 1977), 94.

50 Douglas, 44.

51 Nancy F. Cott et al., "Beyond Roles, Beyond Spheres: Thinking about Gender in the Early Republic," *William and Mary Quarterly* 46 (July 1989): 565-85. This study was originally presented in 1987 at a forum at the Philadelphia Center for Early American Studies at the University of Pennsylvania.

52 Ibid., 567.

53 Ibid., 568.

54 Ibid., 568.

55 Linda K. Kerber, "Separate Spheres, Female Worlds, Woman's Place: The Rhetoric of Women's History," *The Journal of American History* 75, no. 1 (June 1988): 11.

56 David G. Hackett, "Gender and Religion in American Culture, 1870-1930," *Religion and American Culture* 5, no. 2 (Summer 1995): 128-29.

57 Ibid., 133.

58 Mary P. Ryan, *The Empire of the Mother: American Writing about Domesticity, 1830-1860* (New York: The Institute for Research in History and The Haworth Press, 1982), 8.

59 Nancy F. Cott, "On Men's History and Women's History," in *Meanings for Manhood: Construction of Masculinity in Victorian America*, ed. Mark C. Carnes and Clyde Griffen (Chicago and London: The University of Chicago Press, 1990), 207-08.

60 Colleen McDannell, *The Christian Home in Victorian America, 1840-1900* (Bloomington: Indiana University Press, 1986), 108-49.

61 Barbara Welter, "The Cult of True Womanhood: 1800-1860," and "The Feminization of American Religion: 1800-1860," in *Dimity Convictions: The American Woman in the Nineteenth Century* (Athens: Ohio University Press, 1976), 21.

62 Paula Baker, "The Domestication of Politics: Women and American Political Society, 1780-1920," *American Historical Review* 89 (1984): 630.

63 Nancy F. Cott, "Preface to the Second Edition: Then and Since," in *The Bonds of Womanhood: "Woman's Sphere" in New England, 1780-1835* (New Haven and London: Yale University Press, 1997), xii.

64 Bushnell's concept of home will be discussed in detail in Chapter 2, "Women in the Family."

65 E. Anthony Rotundo, *American Manhood: Transformation in Masculinity from the Revolution to the Modern Era* (New York: BasicBooks, 1993).

66 Bushnell's views of men's roles in the family will be discussed in Chapter 2, "Women in the Family."

67 Susan Hill Lindley, *"You Have Stept Out Of Your Place": A History of Women and Religion in America* (Louisville: Westminster John Knox Press, 1996).

68 Barbara Brown Zikmund, "The Struggle for the Right to Preach," in *Women and Religion in America: The Nineteenth Century*, ed. Rosemary Radford Ruether and Rosemary Skinner Keller (San Francisco: Harper & Row, Publishers, 1981), 193-205.

69 Jeannine E. Olson, *One Ministry[,] Many Roles: Deacons and Deaconesses through the Centuries* (St. Louis: Concordia Publishing House, 1992), 19.

70 Leonard I. Sweet, *The Minister's Wife: Her Role in Nineteenth-Century American Evangelicalism* (Philadelphia: Temple University Press, 1983), 3.

71 Lois A. Boyd, "Presbyterian Ministers' Wives: A Nineteenth-Century Portrait," *Journal of Presbyterian History* 59 (1981): 15.

72 Julie Roy Jeffrey, "Ministry Through Marriage: Methodist Clergy Wives on the Trans-Mississippi Frontier," in *Women in New Worlds: Historical Perspectives on the Wesleyan Tradition*, vol. 1, ed. Hilah F. Thomas and Rosemary Skinner Keller (Nashville: Abingdon, 1981), 153.

73 Ellen Carol DuBois, *Feminism and Suffrage: The Emergence of an Independent Women's Movement in America, 1848-1869* (Ithaca and London: Cornell University Press, 1978), 42.

74 Steven M. Buechler, *Women's Movements in the United States: Woman Suffrage, Equal Rights, and Beyond* (New Brunswick and London: Rutgers University Press, 1990), 88.

75 DuBois, 15-202.

76 Carole Nichols, *Votes and More for Women: Suffrage and After in Connecticut* (New York: The Institute for Research in History and The Haworth Press, Inc., 1983).

77 Susan E. Marshall, *Splintered Sisterhood: Gender and Class in the Campaign against Woman Suffrage* (Madison: The University of Wisconsin Press, 1997).

78 Horace Bushnell, *Women's Suffrage; The Reform Against Nature* (New York: Charles Scribner and Company, 1869).

79 Horace Bushnell, *Christian Nurture* (New York: Charles Scribner, 1861; reprint, Grand Rapids: Baker Book House, 1979).

80 *Christian Nurture* became one of the most influential works in Christian theology and Christian education in America. In my view, *Christian Nurture* is important not only in Christian theology and Christian education, but also with regard to its views on women's issues. *Christian Nurture* (1861) developed from the following works published in 1847—*Discourses on Christian Nurture*, "An Argument for *Discourses on Christian Nurture*, Addressed to the Publishing Committee of the Massachusetts Sabbath School Society," and *Views of Christian Nurture, and of Subjects Adjacent Thereto. Discourses on Christian Nurture* (1847) is comprised of two discourses delivered at the North Congregational Church in Hartford in March 1835. *Views of Christian Nurture, and of Subjects Adjacent Thereto* (1847) consists of "Christian Nurture: Discourse I and Discourse II," "Argument for *Discourses on Christian Nurture*," "Spiritual Economy of Revivals of Religion," "Growth, not Conquest, the True method of Christian Progress," "The Organic Unity of the Family," and "The Scene of the Pentecost, and a Christian Parish." "Christian Nurture: Discourse I and Discourse II" is identical to *Discourses on Christian Nurture* in 1847. "Argument for *Discourses on Christian Nurture*" is "An Argument for *Discourses on Christian Nurture*" with a newly written "Note." "Spiritual Economy of Revivals of Religion" is identical to Bushnell's article in *The Quarterly Christian Spectator* in February, 1838. "Growth, Not Conquest, the True method of Christian Progress" is a new title to his article, "The Kingdom of Heaven as a Grain of Mustard Seed" which appeared in *The New Englander* in October, 1844. These works became the basis of *Christian Nurture* in the final 1861 form.

CHAPTER 2
WOMEN IN THE FAMILY

Natures of Women and Men

Men's Government and Women's Subordination

Horace Bushnell desired a Christian America based on the organic unity of family, church, and nation. He hoped to realize this goal by emphasizing the different natures of men and women. Bushnell's theory was that men should govern women, and women should be subordinate to men.[1]

Bushnell affirmed that males should carry out governmental functions,[2] contending that in any form of government—whether it was the family, the church, or the state—the ruling function should belong to men. He decidedly declared, "Man is to govern; all government belongs to men."[3] Hence, the leadership and the decision-power of the house, the church, and the state belonged to males.[4]

Conversely, Bushnell asserted that women should be subordinate to men, and regarded this subordination as "the most honorable, finest, highest nature, in many of its qualities and capabilities it had ever been given us to know."[5] However, he did not explain why he thought that the subordination of women was so honorable, fine, and of the highest nature. He simply declared his position.

Contrary to what one might expect, Bushnell did not think that subordination should mean inferiority. He remarked:

> We Americans take up some very crude notions of subordination, as if it implied inferior quality, character, power. No such thing is true, or less than plainly false. Subordination is one thing, inferiority an immensely different thing.[6]

He, thus, distinguished the notion of subordination from that of inferiority. For him, "subordination" was not a negative term. Rather, he asserted that, due to their nature, women voluntarily should accept their subordinate status.[7]

Biblical Interpretation of Male and Female Natures: Bushnell and Stanton

To support the argument that women should be subordinate to men and men should govern women, Bushnell (a pastoral theologian) made use of the Bible,[8] particularly the Old Testament story of Creation. According to his interpretation, the woman had not been created as the man's duplicate, in other words, as a second man. Instead, Bushnell believed that the woman had been derivative from the man. He also thought that the woman had been created as the "meet-helper" [helpmeet] of the man. In other words, the woman was a being whose nature was subsidiary and complementary to the man.[9]

In his writing, Bushnell focused solely on Chapter 2 of Genesis. He completely ignored Genesis, Chapter 1, a story that describes the simultaneous creation and equality of the man and the woman.

Elizabeth Cady Stanton (1815-1902) was a contemporary of Horace Bushnell and a leader of the women's suffrage movement in nineteenth-century America. She, along with other women, wrote *The Woman's Bible* commentary. It is, therefore, valid to compare Bushnell's interpretation of the story of Creation with Stanton's. In *The Woman's Bible*, Stanton highlighted Chapter 1 of Genesis, and commented on the story of creation. She noted that the Genesis 1 story proclaimed the simultaneous creation of man and woman in the image of God and the equality of both sexes.[10] Stanton also stressed that all the theories based upon the assumption that the male was created prior to the female or that the female was subjected to the male in creation had no scriptural foundation.[11]

Bushnell, on the other hand, believed that the New Testament, as well as the Old Testament, asserted the subordination of women to men.[12] To support his argument, he cited The First Letter to the Corinthians by the Apostle Paul:

> As "the head of every man is Christ," so "the head of the woman is the man;" as "he is the image and [reflected] glory of God," so "the woman is the glory of the man." "For the man is not of the woman, but the woman of the man. Neither was the man created for the woman, but the woman for the man." "The woman is to learn in silence, with all subjection"— "not to teach nor to usurp authority over the man, but to be in silence."[13]

However, Bushnell noted, "These heavy pronouncements of the apostle come down with a kind of pounding emphasis on women, that sounds harshly [*sic*]."[14] He believed that if Paul had been married, the apostle's words would have been more courteous to women; and that if Paul had lived in the nineteenth century, he would not have written so much about the obedience of women.[15] Despite this, Bushnell basically supported the apostle's pronouncements. He wrote:

> He [Paul] is perfectly right in every positive utterance and moral pronouncement he makes. So far he indorses [*sic*] and sanctions the grand first truth of the sexly nature seen by us all; the superior headship of man, and the subordinated, complementary life of woman.[16]

On the other side of the argument, Elizabeth Cady Stanton asserted that educated women should rebel against ideas and customs based upon the supposition of women's "heaven-ordained subjection."[17] She also encouraged women "to be guided by their own unassisted common sense."[18]

Bushnell's reservations about Paul caused him to be much more comfortable with Peter's comments regarding women. In his interpretation of the First Letter of Peter, he noted:

> He [Peter] begins at the same point with Paul—"Likewise ye wives be in subjection to your own husbands." . . . Their husbands may "without the word,"—without preaching, without exhortation—"be won by the conversation [the beautiful way] of their wives."[19]

But, Bushnell went on to add:

> He [Peter] goes on to speak of their [wives'] adorning—which is to be no outward glare of trinkets, and gems, and braidings of hair, and dresses in the mode . . . but it is to be internal worth and beauty, the hidden magic of a dear, celestial character; that which, in God's scale of judgment, is of great price.[20]

Peter's words resonated with Bushnell, who was not favorably disposed toward the externally showy women emerging in his era.

Bushnell's congregation was largely comprised of middle-class people. During the mid-1800s, fashion increasingly became a means by which the upwardly mobile could be either embraced or excluded by the bourgeoisie. Bushnell was among those who felt that character was sacrificed when individuals focused their energies on mere appearance. What made the illusory world of fashion particularly heinous to Bushnell (among others) was that fashion aimed at women who were, as Karen Halttunen notes, also responsible for maintaining the virtue of sincerity, particularly within the sphere of the home.[21] Thus, it should come as no surprise that Bushnell expected women to cultivate internal worth and beauty, rather than the latest styles. He no doubt believed that inner characteristics resulted in a celestial character.

Stanton, however, did not believe that women were the only ones lacking character. Her commentary on the First Letter of Peter stated that "woman's love of satins, of velvets, of lace, and of jewels, had its corresponding expression in man's love of wealth, of position, and his ambition for personal and family aggrandizement."[22] That is, Stanton observed the weak points of men and women equally.

Link to the Issue of Women's Suffrage

Bushnell also linked what he thought Scripture said to the issue of women's suffrage. For instance, he commented:

> The assertion of their [women's] political equality with men would have shocked any apostle, or other scripture writer, and an agitation by women, based on such equality, to secure the right of open contest with men for political office and power, would have been looked upon even as an offense against nature itself—an outrage on decency and order utterly abominable.[23]

For Bushnell, women's suffrage was an offense against the natures of women and men. By utilizing biblical references and the notion of the separate natures of women and men, he thereby rejected women suffrage. The rejection of women's suffrage and other forms of female governance was crucial to his process of building a Christian America.

Marriage

Changing Meaning and Function of Marriage

In mid nineteenth-century New England, society was rapidly changing from an agricultural, "homespun," society to an industrial one. With these changes taking place in New England, the meaning and function of marriage were changing also. In "The Age of Homespun," Bushnell discussed the function and meaning of marriage in the homespun age, which he understood to exist from the middle of the eighteenth century to the middle of the nineteenth century. He commented, "The woman was given to the man to be a help, meet [a helpmeet] for him."[24] He also remarked, "The women are given not so much to help their husbands spend a living, as to help them get one."[25] From Bushnell's point of view, married women in the homespun age helped their husbands to earn a living, while women in the middle of the nineteenth century were not necessarily economic helpers to their husbands. As mentioned earlier, the impact of industrialization meant that the family's economic condition now depended upon the receipt of wages, and wages were something that middle- and upper-class homemakers did not receive for their services. Bushnell was one of the persons who reacted negatively to changes in a culture that now encouraged wives to become consumers and spend their husbands' income.

Alternative Ideas and Practices of Marriage

Nineteenth-century America saw the rise of alternative religions advocating ideas and practices different from traditional views and practices of marriage. For instance, Mormons practiced polygamy, Shakers insisted on celibacy, and the Oneida Community practiced "complex marriage," which provided sexual variety and satisfaction without the risks of pregnancy.[26]

Barbara Welter points out another interesting change regarding nineteenth-century American marriage. She states that although marriage was considered to be the best state for a woman, it was not thought to be absolutely essential.[27] Carl N. Degler also notes that women who never married increased over the course of the nineteenth century.[28]

Thus, nineteenth-century women were presented with alternative lifestyles that did not include marriage and/or provided relationships other than the traditional one man and one woman structure. They also responded to the alternatives. One such response resulted in an increase in the number of single females.

Bushnell's Views on Marriage

Horace Bushnell, however, could not conceive of women and men who chose to remain unmarried. He valued the traditional form of marriage and saw it as a crucial institution. Additionally, he believed women and men could actualize their natures through matrimony. In other words, in marriage, men could actualize their governing nature, and women could realize their subordinate nature. From Bushnell's point of view, the actualization of both sexes' natures in marriage created a solid foundation for the family and contributed to the sanctum of the larger social order.

Bushnell believed that marriage was completely different from a mere partnership contract. He stated:

> The two [man and woman] come together not to be one, a total nature, which is marriage, but to be two in equal contract, which is partnership. Of course the partnership contract may be terminated, as all other contracts may, by the parties themselves.[29]

He, therefore, did not agree with the idea of contract marriage. He reasoned that there should be a head in marriage; whereas, there was no head in a partnership contract. Thus, the difference between marriage and a partnership contract was whether or not a head existed. Bushnell explained:

> Is there not a man and woman, and are not the two a complete one? And is not the man as visibly head of that oneness as any head set upon two shoulders was ever head of the body? Partnerships have no head in this way, because the ditto principle exactly levels the parties. Marriage has and is to have, must have, a head, and a connecting bond that runs down through.[30]

From his perspective, women and men were ideal wives and husbands when they actualized their essential natures. For Bushnell, ideal wives fit the following description:

> Young gentleman of homespun thinks of a wife, not of a holiday partner who may come into his living in a contract of expenditure. He believes in woman according to God's own idea, looks to her as an angel of help, who may join herself to him, and go down the rough way of life as it is, to strengthen him in it by her sympathy, and gild its darkness, if dark it must be, by the light of her patience and the constancy of her devotion.[31]

So, ideal wives were not temporary contract partners who agreed to spend their husbands' income, but "angels of help." They were sympathetic, patient, and devoted. It is also clear that even though the above quotation focused on the ideal wife of the homespun age, Bushnell was in reality describing his image of the ideal wife of his own era.

In addition, Bushnell describes the image of an ideal wife by utilizing his experiences with his own wife. For instance, from 1847 until 1853, he was accused of being a heretic because his books *Christian Nurture*, *God in Christ*, and *Christ in Theology* were so controversial. During this most difficult time of his life, his wife shared his suffering with him. Thus, he came to portray her as someone who gave him strength.[32]

Bushnell's image of the ideal wife, furthermore, closely resembled the image of Jesus Christ's passion and resurrection. Whenever he discussed women's issues, Christ's suffering and resurrection emerged both implicitly and explicitly. For example, from Bushnell's perspective, what his wife (the ideal wife) did for/with him was similar to what Jesus Christ did for/with him in His suffering and resurrection. Put another way, Bushnell's wife suffered for him and with him (especially when he was accused of heresy) and helped him emerge from the death of controversy and disgrace into a new life.

Horace Bushnell looked upon a monogamous marital relationship as very important. In *Christian Nurture*, he cited Malachi 2:15, which says, "And did he not make one? Yet, had he the residue of the Spirit. And wherefore one? That he might have a godly seed." Bushnell offered the following explanation of the verse:

> The prophet is enforcing here a strict observance of marriage. And he adverts, in his argument, to the single and sole state of the first human pair, as a standing proof against polygamy, inconstancy, and all similar abuses of the marriage state.[33]

It is no surprise, then, that Bushnell decidedly rejected the idea of polygamy and infidelity in married life. Rather, he affirmed a monogamous marital relationship that was expected to last throughout the couple's life.

Characteristics of Bushnell's Views of Marriage

Bushnell's views of marriage, therefore, had four characteristics. First, he thought that it was natural for men and women to marry and that marriage should last until death divided the husband and the wife. Additionally, since he believed that marriage was the vehicle through which men and women could realize their true natures, Bushnell did not seem to value the single state in life. Second, he did not regard marriage in terms of a partnership contract between men and women because, in his view, the idea of a contract suggested that the marriage could be terminated in much the same way that a business relationship could be terminated. Third, based on his belief that men were created to govern and women to be subordinate, Bushnell thought a husband should function as the head of the marital relationship. Fourth, as mentioned previously, his image of the ideal wife closely resembled the image of Jesus Christ in his suffering and resurrection. All of these characteristics make it clear that Bushnell understood marriage, not as an egalitarian partnership, but as a protective-subordinate structure.

Bushnell's Marriage Ceremony

Did Bushnell's views of marriage shape the ceremony he officiated over as a pastor of the North Congregational Church in Hartford? By examining his marriage ceremony, one can see how his views of marriage were worked out in practice.

Horton Davies notes that there was no single, exclusive and official form of marriage service for Congregationalists.[34] Davies, however, explains that the essentials of a Congregational marriage service did include the following:

> Reminders of the purposes of Christian marriage in an opening exhortation and in NT lessons; the charge that any impediments to the marriage be openly declared; the affirmations of mutual loyalty made by groom and bride; the mutual pledging of their troth and the exchange of rings; the minister's pronouncement in the triune name of God that bride and groom are married; and prayers and hymns for the keeping of the promises made and for the building of a Christian home, with the divine assistance, concluding with the Lord's Prayer and the blessing.[35]

Bushnell's style of performing a marriage ceremony—what he inserted into or deleted from the basic format above—yields concrete clues regarding his views of marriage.[36] First of all, he would declare to the parties, "This rite of marriage in which you twain come now to be united, as in bonds of religion, is the first and oldest rite of the world." He would then ask the man, "Will you . . . promise to keep, cherish, and defend her and to be her faithful and true husband so long as you both shall live?" Next, Bushnell would inquire of the woman, "Will you . . . promise to adhere unchangeably to him in all life's changes, and to be his loving and true wife till death divide you?" In the ring ceremony, he would say:

> Forasmuch now as the husband is the head of the wife, imparting unto her his name and receiving her into his care and providence, I give you [the man] this ring that you may place it on the finger of this woman, as a token that in troth you so receive her.[37]

After the ring was placed on the woman's finger, Bushnell would read the following:

> Thus are *you* to compass about her life with strength and protecting love. Thus are *you* to wear this ring as the enclosing bond of reverence and dearest faith, both fulfilling the perfect circle of duty that makes you one.[38]

He would pronounce the man and the women to be husband and wife, and finally add, "What God hath joined together, let no man put asunder."

If we compare Bushnell's style of a marriage ceremony with the essentials of marriage ceremonies for Congregationalists provided by Davies, we can see that Bushnell's marriage ceremony appears to be traditional and/or conventional. However, his marriage ceremony seems to have three principles. First, the husband should defend or protect the wife, and be the head of the marital union. Second, the wife should adhere to the husband. Third, married life should last until death divided the husband and the wife.

Bushnell's style of marriage ceremony, therefore, corresponded with his views on marriage. In addition, his style of marriage ceremony and his views on marriage coincided with his basic views of the different natures of men and women (men's government of women and women's subordination to men).

Women's Roles in Christian Nurture

Bushnell desired a Christian America, the corner stone for which was the institution of family as well as those of church and nation. He thought that the parental nurturing of children, and in particular the nurturing of children from the perspective of Christian values, was crucial to the stability and prosperity of the American family, church, and nation.

"The Age of Homespun" and *Christian Nurture*

Bushnell delivered the discourse, "The Age of Homespun," at the Centennial Celebration of Litchfield County, Connecticut, in 1851. One of the characteristics of "The Age of Homespun" is that Bushnell portrayed men as generally uninvolved in the Christian nurture of children. Instead, he presented mothers as the main nurturers.

"The Age of Homespun" (1851) and *Christian Nurture* (1861) illustrate a difference in Bushnell's understanding of the roles of fathers and mothers. When he wrote *Christian Nurture*, Bushnell charged both mothers and fathers with the nurture of their children.

Analyses of Bushnell's Views on *Christian Nurture*

Despite the above, most scholars have suggested that Bushnell placed the overwhelming importance on the responsibility of mothers to nurture their children into Christian maturity. However, in *Christian Nurture*, it seems clear that Bushnell thought the opportunity and responsibility for the Christian nurture of children was almost equal between fathers and mothers. Additionally, in the matters of family prayer and family government, he placed much more emphasis on fathers than on mothers. Thus, his views about the roles of fathers and mothers in the family's Christian nurture corresponded with his position on the hierarchically complementary roles of men and women. Furthermore, men in *Christian Nurture* were given important roles in raising Christian children.

David G. Hackett notes that the separation of the home from the workplace resulted in the creation of a separate women's sphere in Victorian America. This separation had the effect of removing the father from the strong currents of feeling that flowed between generations in the family.[39]

However, Hackett's observation does not apply to the ideal fathers and mothers that Bushnell presented in *Christian Nurture*. Bushnell did not remove fathers from the family, but in fact encouraged them to participate in the raising of their children. *Christian Nurture* told men to embrace the opportunities and responsibilities for nurturing children as fathers, even as it instructed women to do the same as mothers. Bushnell's *Christian Nurture* is filled with concrete examples of opportunities and responsibilities for both parents.

Ronald William Hogeland writes that both domestic reform literature and Bushnell completely excluded fathers from any responsibility regarding their children's nurture.[40] Yet I found that Bushnell clearly did not exclude the father from the family at all in *Christian Nurture*.[41]

However, some scholars have noticed that both sexes participated in nineteenth-century American family life. Mary P. Ryan points out that the family in the nineteenth century was built on a heterosexual union between husband and wife. She comments, "Even if the nineteenth-century home was infused with feminine values or dominated by the psychological influence of the mother, its fundamental structure was woven of heterosexual relationships."[42] Nancy F. Cott has also argued that male influence was not absent from the home. She observes that men held legal and patriarchal power, and their domination over the home was even more enforced legally than was their domination over political and economic areas in the nineteenth-century America.[43]

Although paternal roles in *Christian Nurture* differ somewhat from the notion of male domination with its absolute power, I agree with Cott's statement that men were not absent from the Christian nurturing process. In *Christian Nurture,* Bushnell presented an ideal in which men (fathers) actually seem to be much more responsible for nurturing the children of the family than women (mothers).

Colleen McDannell presents two models of education, worship, and government that were present in Victorian American family life (1840-1900): the paternal model and the maternal model. With regard to the paternal model, McDannell writes that the father was head of the household. Therefore, education, worship and government in the family were his responsibilities.[44] However, in the maternal model, the mother and children became the focus of the family, while the father and his responsibilities toward the family existed on the periphery.[45]

Based on McDanell's two models, it seems that Bushnell's understanding belonged to both the paternal model and the maternal model, even though most scholars regard Bushnell as a representative of only the maternal model. My research also reveals that Bushnell clearly favored the paternal model with regard to family prayer and government.

Bushnell's understanding of manhood is also important to his concept of family life. E. Anthony Rotundo has divided the history of manhood in America into three general transformational phases.[46] The first phase was communal manhood. The second and the third were respectively self-made manhood, and passionate manhood. Rotundo begins the first phase in colonial New England and extends it into the first decade of the nineteenth century. He notes that for early New Englanders, the essence of manhood was located in the man's role as head of the household.[47] Rotundo continues, "The head of the household was the embodiment of all its members. . . . The head of the family was its link to community governance. He was the household's voting representative in public councils."[48] In a family, the head of the household led the rest of the family in daily worship.[49]

During the communal manhood phase, the family was the primary unit of production, the fundamental unit of society, and the basic unit of the political system.[50] In addition, Rotundo notes that the family was supposed to be mirrored in governmental structure, and that the government was supposed to be mirrored in the family's structure.[51] People thought of their society as "organic." Terms such as "individuality" or "self-reliance" had little place in this first phase of communal manhood.[52]

Rotundo calls the second phase the period of self-made manhood, and notes that it began to grow in the late eighteenth century.[53] The notion of self-made manhood emerged as part of a broader series of changes, including the birth of republican government, the spread of a market economy, and the concomitant growth of the middle class. Men were expected to fulfill themselves through personal success in business and the professions.[54] This notion of self-made manhood reflected "the new era of individualism."[55] As a result, Rotundo notes, the pursuit of self-interest began to tear apart the social fabric, and society came to be seen as a collection of individuals.[56]

In addition, Rotundo writes that the reduction of the fathers' status in the nineteenth-century American family was due to a dramatic enlargement of the mothers' parenting role; and that for the first time in American history, the mother had become the primary parent.[57] My reading of *Christian Nurture*, however, does not confirm that Bushnell held Rotundo's general view of the roles of fathers and mothers. Rather, it seems that Bushnell refused to embrace the societal changes that reduced the father's role in the family and that placed the burden of family life solely upon the shoulders of the mother.

According to Rotundo, the third phase, passionate manhood, arose in the late nineteenth century. Passionate manhood was a variation of self-made manhood. However, male passions such as ambition, combativeness, competitiveness, aggression, and toughness were especially valued in this phase. At the same time, play and leisure entertainment began to gain approval as men's activities. Men were starting to define their identities not just in the workplace but outside of it as well.[58]

On the basis of these interpretive schemes for understanding manhood in American history, the ideal fathers presented by Bushnell in *Christian Nurture* are not the self-made men of the early-to-mid-nineteenth century. Rather, they seem to be the communal men of the previous phase—a phase which Rotundo says lasted from the colonial era until the early nineteenth century. Therefore, one can say that Bushnell preferred the earlier model of manhood to the emerging models of his own era.

Only three scholars, to date, have noticed that Bushnell placed almost equal importance on fatherhood and motherhood in *Christian Nurture*. John M. Mulder has commented that Bushnell was "remarkably evenhanded" in *Christian Nurture* regarding paternal and maternal religious obligations.[59] In addition, Jerry W. McCant notes that the model of nurture presented by Bushnell was not entirely maternal.[60] In fact, McCant makes the observation that Bushnell's chapter on ostrich nurture called mothers into accountability, but at the same time did not allow fathers to think that they were free from blame. McCant adds:

> Note that even in the young years of infancy, Bushnell envisioned the involvement of both the father and mother in the process of nurturance. Reflecting on his own times, the mother is seen as perhaps more involved, but Christian nurture was not seen as a solo project![61]

He goes on to clearly state:

> No one can deny the importance of the mother in Bushnell's schemata of Christian nurture. However, given the times in which he wrote, one is struck by the balance in his discussion of the religious duties of both mothers and fathers in Christian nurture. His consistent plural use of the word *parent* emphasizes that he did not advocate the father's abdication of his responsibilities to the child.[62]

Furthermore, in his recent article, Mark Edwards writes that both parents in *Christian Nurture* are charged with the Christian nurturing of their children. He writes, "Gender-neutral language such as 'you,' the 'parents,' and 'the Christian parent' were employed throughout his [Bushnell's] treatise."[63]

These three scholars, then, support my perception that Bushnell viewed the roles of fathers and mothers as equally important. In fact, Bushnell often used the term "Christian parents" when writing *Christian Nurture*. His word choice makes it clear that he was advising fathers as well as mothers to participate in the nurture of their children. Bushnell wrote, "Both the parents should be truly in them together, and the children carefully bred into them also as the common joy of their home."[64]

In certain discussions in *Christian Nurture*, however, Bushnell uses the terms "mothers" and "fathers" individually, rather than the term "Christian parents." That distinction is not unimportant, for it includes certain significant points. For instance, Bushnell placed women on a pedestal in *Christian Nurture*, and regarded their maternal affection as semi-divine. He remarked:

> Some highest and most sacred office of motherhood were required to begin. . . . If she could sound her consciousness deeply enough, she would find a certain religiousness in it [the inborn personality]. Here springs the secret of her maternity, and its semi-divine proportions. It is the call and equipment of God, for a work on the impressional and plastic age of a soul. Christianized as it should be, and wrought in by the grace of the Spirit, the minuteness of its care, its gentleness, its patience, its almost divine faithfulness, are prepared for the shaping of a soul's immortality. . . . This motherhood may more certainly plant the angel in the man, uniting him to all heavenly goodness by predispositions from itself.[65]

According to Bushnell, then, maternal affection was semi-divine because it was "the call and equipment of God" given to women to shape the soul of young children. Through semi-divine maternal affection, the children were "united to all heavenly goodness." From Bushnell's point of view, fathers had little to do with nurturing children in their "impressional and plastic" period.

In addition, Bushnell expected the role of mothers, rather than that of fathers, to include raising the children to become pious persons. He based this expectation on the biblical case of Timothy:

> Timothy's father was a Greek, (Acts 16: 1) and probably an unbeliever; but his mother was a woman of such piety, that she omitted nothing in the training of her son, and the apostle speaks of her, in the same epistle, even as having let down upon him a kind of piety by entail. But her faithful lessons—these are what he is now calling to mind; and it is affecting to notice that he not only charges it on him to remember what he has learned from the Scriptures, because they are God's word, but also to value the same things the more, "knowing of whom he has learned them;" that is, from his gracious and faithful mother.[66]

In spite of his expectation that mothers should raise their children as pious persons, Bushnell's views of their role in family prayers were complex. First of all, he thought that children should be inducted into the ways and habits of praying by themselves. He observed that Christian mothers prayed too much for their children, and that this practice would not teach the children to pray on their own.[67] Bushnell, therefore, advised mothers "to word a simple prayer for them [the children] herself, and let them follow after in the repetition of it, sentence by sentence."[68] However, the reason a child, particularly a son, needed to be able to pray independently was not merely for personal piety. Bushnell advised, "When the father was absent, or was taken away by death, he [the son] would be ready, at a very early period on his way to manhood, to take his father's place [in leading family prayer]."[69] This comment suggests that the mother's role in family prayer was subsidiary. In Bushnell's mind, the father had the primary responsibility for family prayer. Therefore, when the father could not perform his responsibility, the one to take over family prayer should not be the wife, but the son (the father's surrogate). McDannell also calls attention to this point by noting:

> Even Horace Bushnell, who encouraged mothers to teach their children the basics of prayer, assumed that this early training eventually would allow the "child" to take the father's place at family prayer if he was absent or "taken away by death."[70]

In addition, Bushnell believed that the authority of the father should be present in family government. He explained, "It [family government] is not to be a mere nursing, or dressing, or provisioning agency; not to be an exhorting, advising, consulting relationship; not to be a lavishing of devotion, or parental self-sacrifice."[71] He added, "It [family government] governs, uses authority, maintains law and rules, by a binding and loosing power, over the moral nature of the child."[72] The father, therefore, needed to make use of his governing nature to ensure that the family structure was strong and that rules were enforced. The alternative to this model, Bushnell warned, was the ungoverned family—"the synonym of a disorderly, wretched, and dishonored, if not ruined, family."[73]

Bushnell's view of the mother's role in family government was as complex as his view of family prayer. He believed that government—whether family government, church government, or state government—belonged to men, not women. However, in reality, Bushnell gave governmental roles to women in the first stage of family government. He remarked, "When she [the mother] begins to speak her soft imperative, putting a little decision into the tones of her love, she makes the first and gentlest possible beginning of authority."[74] Bushnell explained that the father's role of family government was to begin with the next stage of the child's life. He wrote:

> The stiffer tension of the masculine word, connected with the wider, rougher providence of a father's masculine force, follows in a stouter mode of authority, and the moral nature of the child, configured thereto, answers faithfully in a rapidly developed sense of obligation.[75]

Therefore, Bushnell expected mothers to use authoritative power in a gentle, yet commanding way, and encouraged fathers to use their authority in a manly and more powerful way. This approach was crucial, particularly in response to the outrageous and shocking misconduct of some boys. In such cases, Bushnell expected fathers to make full use of their authority as persons who represented God, and who were God's ministers.[76]

At the other end of the spectrum, Bushnell appreciated the mother's roles in making the house attractive and pleasant. He wrote:

> It will be the duty of the parents, and a kind of study especially of the mother, to find methods of making the house no mere prison, but a place of attraction, and of always cheerful and pleasant society. . . . Here is the field of the mother's greatest art.[77]

Many scholars have understood Bushnell to be a man who seldom regarded motherhood as negative. However, he had negative attitudes toward women who left the nurturing of their children to others. In Bushnell's era, wealthier people often left the education of their children in the hands of nurses and attendants, even though—according to Bushnell—young children needed the attention and teaching of their mothers.[78] He also pointed out that there were some mothers who did not accept their child willingly,[79] and suggested that this lack of acceptance could happen for the following reasons:

> This charge is going to detain her at home, and limit her freedom. Or it will take her away from the shows and pleasures for which she is living. Or it will burden her days and nights with cares that weary her self-indulgence. Or she is not fond of children, and never means to be fond of them—they are not worth the trouble they cost.[80]

Bushnell also deplored the cruelties that mothers put upon children. For example, he complained that mothers easily fell into the prolongation of punishment.[81] He, furthermore, observed that some women were "nervously anxious mothers." He sympathized with the plight of children who had such mothers by lamenting, "What is the woe put upon a hapless child, who is shut up day by day and year by year, to the always fearing look and deprecating whine, the questioning, protesting, super-cautionary keeping of a nervously anxious mother."[82]

In conclusion, despite the opinions of many scholars, Bushnell actually did not place overwhelming emphasis on the importance of the mother's role in the development of their children. Rather, in *Christian Nurture,* he assigned equal importance on the roles of the mother and father in nurturing the family's children. He did, however, distinguish fatherhood from motherhood, both in family prayers and family government, in a complex way. With regard to family prayers, he expected mothers to assume the role and responsibility in the initial stage of the children's prayer life. The role of mothers, however, was to be subsidiary to the role of fathers in terms of how the family prayers should be conducted. The mother was to train the children how to pray, but the father was to lead the family prayer. In addition, if Bushnell consistently followed his ideas regarding the natures of women and men, he should not have expected mothers to assume any role at all in the area of family government. Nevertheless, he allowed mothers to assume the responsibility of authority in the early stages of family government, primarily with regard to the discipline and teaching of young children. Thus, regarding family prayer and family government, the roles of mother and father were interrelated in complexity: Bushnell assumed that the father's role was much more extensive than that of mother, but maintained a subsidiary position for the mother. This corresponds with Bushnell's belief that a solid family could be formed by reinforcing the hierarchically complementary roles of men and women—in other words, by accepting men's governmental function and women's subordinate function.

Relationships with Family Members

Bushnell's Mother

Bushnell's description of his mother, Dotha, in "God's Way with a Soul,"[83] and "Sketches of His Grandmother and Mother"[84] gives some significant clues as to how he perceived women and motherhood. He wrote, "My mother . . . was of a naturally retiring disposition. . . . Her slender person, her gray-blue eye and softly tinted complexion, indicated a certain fragility and fineness of mould."[85] This image of his own mother became Bushnell's ideal throughout his life in terms of the physical appearance of women. Ideal women were like his mother: retiring, slender, fair, fragile, and fine. In fact, Bushnell actually feared that women would begin to resemble men in appearance, particularly if they entered the political arena and adopted the aggressive behavior of men. Throughout his life, therefore, Horace Bushnell was interested in women's appearance.[86]

He reminisced warmly about his mother, noting, "My God and my good mother both heard the cry [my cry] and went to the task of strengthening and comforting me together, and were able ere long to get a smile upon my face. My mother's loving instinct was from God."[87] Hence, he linked the love of his mother with the love of God.

To Bushnell, his mother was the model of a religious woman. He stated that she preached to the children, not by artificial manners, but by "her maternal sacrifices."[88] The concept of maternal sacrifice was crucial for him. He believed that sacrifice was the very core of the religious nature of women.[89] Furthermore, Bushnell knew that his mother's concern was above all focused on developing her children as strong Christians and having her sons prepare for the Christian ministry.[90] He observed:

> I have seen a great many tokens that she loved the kingdom of Christ, and wanted nothing so much as to have her sons enlisted in its propagation. She also had the satisfaction of seeing two of her sons, the oldest and the youngest, consecrated thus to the special service of her Master.[91]

Bushnell valued the fact that his mother's sphere was her family. He wrote, "Her field was in her family, and there it was that she won her best honors and proved the superiority which everybody felt in her character."[92] His experience of his mother made him confident that women in general would win their best honors within their families and if they focused on their roles as mothers and wives. However, when he discussed contemporary women, Bushnell's opinions about their proper sphere were often blurred, for he considered both home and work place to be appropriate spheres for the women of his time.[93]

Through the lens of Bushnell's daughter, one can gain further insight as to how he viewed his mother. His daughter writes that, "He [Bushnell] spoke to us [his daughters], as often before, of his good and wise mother, the notable housewife and care-taker, the discreet adviser and patient manager of wayward boyhood."[94] Through his views of his mother, therefore, one can see that his expectations of women as mothers included many aspects—wise mother, housewife, care-taker, adviser, and manager within the home.

Bushnell's Father and Fathers in *Christian Nurture*

Bushnell, however, did not write about his father, Ensign, except to comment that his father whipped him only once. Contrary to twenty-first-century expectations, he remembered the discipline as one of the best things that ever happened to him.[95] His personal experience appears to have led him to believe that discipline was important for children. Moreover, he regarded discipline as a crucial part of a father's responsibility in the family.

Although Bushnell did not write about his father, fathers were always present with women and mothers in *Christian Nurture*. This observation is very different from the general view of male and female roles, status, and spheres in nineteenth-century American families provided by scholars such as David G. Hackett, E. Anthony Rotundo and Ronald Hogeland, and will be discussed, in greater detail, later in this chapter.

Bushnell's Ideal Family and His Actual Family

As noted earlier, Bushnell ideally wanted to build a solid family by men's government of women and women's subordination to men. However, in his own family life, he did not try to realize his ideal. In this sense, his views of women in the family showed complexity between the ideal and the actual.

Bushnell's relationships with his immediate family were not those of government. Rather, he sought equality and cooperation with his wife, and provided nurture for his daughters. He clearly did not expect his wife to be subordinate to him. Rather, he wished to grow with his wife, hand in hand, as a husband and a father. Nor did Bushnell ask his daughters to be subject to their father. Rather, in his letters, he encouraged his daughters to become intellectually and religiously cultivated women. His views on women were, therefore, egalitarian and nurturing in his immediate family.

Bushnell's Poor Health Shaped His Relationships with Family

Due to his poor health, Bushnell was often forced to spend periods of time away from home seeking more favorable climatic conditions. According to Ronald William Hogeland, about one-third to one-half of Bushnell's time was spent away from his family from 1839 through 1874.[96] Robert L. Edwards reveals that the reason Bushnell felt compelled to change climates was due to "an undiagnosed tuberculosis" that caused him to become frail and made him appear old before his time.[97] In addition, Edwards explains, "Tuberculosis, one of the killer diseases of the period, intermittently afflicted [Bushnell] with hacking coughs, low fevers, and sieges of what seemed to be flu or common colds, voice problems, and onsets of depression."[98] In 1835, when he was thirty-three years old, just after he entered his ministry, Bushnell began to suffer from throat trouble. In 1839, he wrote to his wife, "I cannot but feel a degree of anxiety about myself in regard to my future health, which is constantly acting on my love to my family. This disease hangs about me, and I am afraid is getting a deeper hold of me."[99]

On April 17, 1845, Bushnell wrote a rather melancholy letter to his wife from North Carolina:

> My heart was oppressed by the thought of my dear family,—how little I had done for them which possibly I might, what must be their condition if my health was indeed finally broke, how I could leave them if I must leave the world. Such thoughts haunted me all the way. . . . I never travelled in such a mood before,—realizing at once my weakness, my shattered state, as never in my whole sickness; and the deep tenderness of my love to you, its strong necessity, its inextinguishable power, as never before in my life.[100]

In 1855, Bushnell was in Cuba and penned these words to his daughter:

> I ought not conceal it from my friends, least of all from my family, that I encounter some discouragements and sometimes am pressed with sore struggles. When my prospect of living is darkened in this manner, I need not tell you how fondly, or with what tender clinging, I remember my dear family, and how these form images that are painted in the inmost chamber of my heart. . . . These four [Bushnell's wife and three daughters] do none the less appear to circumscribe my love and claim it all. When I think of leaving the world, these meet me as my charge, my care, and I long to know what is to befall them.[101]

Thus, his health was one of the important factors that helped shape the relationships between Bushnell and his wife, and between Bushnell and his daughters. On the one hand, his poor health caused him to view his own life pessimistically. Yet, it also left him totally dependent on the care of God. As Bushnell noted in 1855:

> I know not what to say of my health. I am sometimes greatly discouraged, struggle darkly with my symptoms, half let go of my confidence, return with difficulty to my expectations, and finally end with yielding myself to the fatherly sovereignty, falling into it and burying in it all my thoughts, misgivings, cares, and throes. . . . I begin to think now that nothing will cure me but faith, a bath in the supernatural and healing grace of Christ, an inhalation of the Divine Spirit and his new-creating power.[102]

Therefore, because he sensed the fragility of his health, he built strong home-centered relationships with his wife and his daughters, and threw himself on the mercy of his God.

Bushnell and His Wife: A Home-Centered Relationship

During his marriage, Bushnell wrote over one hundred letters to his wife, Mary. These letters reveal, first of all, that he could not conceive of his wife without the notion of motherhood and the concept of home. To Bushnell, the notions of wifehood, motherhood, and home were closely connected. The letter to his wife on September 7, 1839 clearly reveals this connection:

> I am enjoying a very pleasant time here, of course; but not so pleasant that my mind does not often turn towards my dear home, and the dear wife in whom my heart has so sweet a repose. My home is more a home to me than it ever was. I linger round it with a domestic love which I seem never to have realized before, except in some partial degree. Perhaps it is owing partly to the plans we have been moulding together for the advancement of our children, the disinterested and somewhat self-denying expedients we have been projecting. But wife and Children,—a wife the dearer because she is the mother of my children; children the dearer because they are the children of my wife; home sanctified by the common endearments of both,—these are the thoughts and images that visit me with their fresh and gentle influence.[103]

Based on the above letter, Bushnell drew a picture of home that consisted of a mother (wife), a father (husband), and their children. In a home, a husband's heart could find rest in his wife; and a wife and a husband together could nurture their children. In addition, Bushnell perceived the home to be a sanctified place.

Regarding the first matter, or the matter of a husband in a home, Bushnell noted, "The masculine half-being [the man or the husband] must be allowed to sink into the bigger self that he calls his home, and be sheltered in the womanly peace [in the carefulness, the love and the beauty of woman] he had protected."[104] It is clear and concrete that Bushnell saw women's carefulness, love, and beauty to be a shelter for men. It is also clear that, from Bushnell's point of view, husbands were supposed to protect their wives from the world. However, he did not provide concrete descriptions of how men were supposed to protect their wives. The second matter, that a wife and a husband (a mother and a father in a home) together should nurture their children, has already been discussed in a previous section of this chapter.

Furthermore, Bushnell thought that a home should be a place "sanctified" by God, as well as sweet and comfortable. In the letter dated August 8, 1842, he referred to his home as "my own sweet, blessed home."[105] He went on to write, "Never did I seem to see so feelingly that our house and home is the place for us, and that God is specially to be thanked for its comfort and its sweet enjoyments."[106] With regard to this idea of home, Bushnell noted, "Home and religion are kindred words . . . home, because it is the seat of religion; religion, because it is the sacred element of home."[107] Thus, he saw home and religion organically linked together. Each was related to the other, and each made important contributions to the other.

To sum up, Bushnell thought that home was a place for a husband to protect his wife and children from the world; a place for a husband to rest in a wife's loving care; the location in which a father and a mother, hand in hand, nurtured their children; and the place that was the seat of religion (in Bushnell's case, Christianity). All of these constitute the primary characteristics of his concept of home.

Bushnell recognized and appreciated the ways in which his wife influenced him. In 1844 he wrote these words to Mary:

> Never did I realize so convincingly the great power you have over me, and how necessary you are to my well-being. . . . It [Charm of power] is not an ambitious, noisy power; it is silent, calm, persuasive, and often so deep as to have its hold deeper than consciousness itself.[108]

Hence, he understood that his wife influenced him, not in an ambitious, noisy manner, but in a calm, strong, silent way. He did not endorse nor did he support women who appeared ambitious and outspoken. This suggests that Bushnell found the silent Mary (the mother of Jesus) to be the model of the ideal woman. In later life, he opposed women who forcefully and ambitiously advocated women's suffrage. These women were too noisy and too worldly for him, and did not meet his understanding of the female ideal.

Bushnell looked upon his wife as an angel. In an 1844 letter, he wrote, "We hear a great deal of maids who are angels, but to me the truest angels on earth are the good wives."[109] In his opinion, the concept of wives (women) as angels was a key and positive notion, and he viewed his own beloved wife in this way.[110]

Bushnell and His Wife: Minister and Minister's Wife in Their Relationship—The Christly Spirit

After his return to America from Europe, the relationship between Bushnell and his wife was not only a home-centered relationship between husband and wife, but also a relationship between minister and minister's wife. That is, they were comrades, "fellow soldiers for Christianity," who were engaged in "the common errand"[111] God gave them. The following excerpt from a letter written in 1852 shows Bushnell's attitude regarding this relationship. He explained:

> Oh what a blessed and complete union will two such find when they come out together . . . to participate in the common triumph of their warfare! Let it be our chief thing, for the rest of life, to stimulate and help each other, and fulfil the common errand [their ministry of Christianity] God has given us."[112]

He, therefore, not only understood himself as a minister, but also expected his wife to join with him in ministry.[113]

A central topic in Bushnell's letters to his wife was "the Christly spirit."[114] He wrote to her in 1852, "Have we so great a joy, my dear wife, so close at hand? Let it be a joy baptized in our faith, our spiritual oneness and purity, as the loving children of God."[115] In 1855, Bushnell wrote to his wife from Cuba, "May our God unite us all in the dearest bonds of holiness and duty, and, by all his discipline of trial and the separations he calls us to suffer, purify us to a more complete love and fellowship with himself."[116] Thus, he saw both joys and difficulties as forms of purification that united them, not only as husband and wife, but also as fellow Christians.

Although most scholars have not mentioned the spiritual aspect of the relationship between Bushnell and his wife, Bushnell regarded the Christ-like spirit as important in the marital relationship. This appears to be one of the most important characteristics of the relationship between the Bushnells.

How did Bushnell learn the importance of the "Christly spirit?" As his wife explained, Bushnell experienced Christianity at a deeper level in 1848.[117] That experience came not as something reasoned out, but as an inspiration or a revelation from God.[118] Earlier, in 1842, the Bushnells had lost their only son, and this set Bushnell on a spiritual journey. Regarding the episode, his wife commented, "God had spoken personally to him in the death of his beloved little boy, drawing his thought and affections to the spiritual and unseen, until, by slow advances, the heavenly vision burst upon him."[119] Around 1848, Bushnell was reading devotional literature, in particular the writings of the seventeenth-century French archbishop, Francois Fenelon (1651-1715), and Thomas C. Upham's biography of Fenelon's quietist contemporary, Madame Guyon (1648-1717).[120] Bushnell wrote that Madame Guyon found God's inspiration and entered into the secret of God's will. She then opened her understandings of God's mysteries to Francois Fenelon.[121] Interestingly enough, Bushnell also referred to Guyon at the very end of *Women's Suffrage.* Robert Mullin writes, "The same writer who had most profoundly affected [Bushnell] years earlier was now invoked as a true role model for women."[122] That is, Bushnell applied the mystic spirituality of Guyon to the religious nature of all women. In this way, Bushnell's own spiritual experiences and his encounters with devotional writings led him to understand God as mysterious and caused him to realize the importance of the spiritual dimension. Judging from his writing, then, the mysterious and spiritual aspects of Christianity had a profound impact on Bushnell, surfacing in his theological work and also in his marital relationship with his wife.

Bushnell and His Wife: An Equal Relationship

In a letter written to his wife just after his retirement from the North Congregational Church, Bushnell referred to her as "feminine Providence."[123] He told her that:

> I got your letter of expostulation, remonstrance, etc., this noon. . . . I am affected by the tender, always wifely, care of me shown by your letters, and none the less that you lecture me a little in your watchfulness. . . . The watch of

> a wife is a very close one, and sublimely tireless,—a kind of feminine Providence that never sleeps.[124]

This letter illustrates that in actuality Bushnell's wife was not innocently quiet. She reasoned earnestly and even protested or argued with her husband. He obviously depended upon her to nudge him into correct behavior and thought.

Based upon the above information, there seems to be no evidence that Bushnell governed his wife, nor that his wife was forced to be subordinate. It is clear that in real life their relationship was not a governing-subordinate one, but rather was one that endorsed equality.

Bushnell and His Daughters: His Expectations

Bushnell wrote more than twenty letters to his daughters during the years from 1843 until 1870. Although he sent letters like journals to his wife from Europe in 1845, he also wrote, in that same year, the most important of his letters to his daughters from Europe. The following letter began with "My dear child," but it is clear that Bushnell was writing to his first daughter, Frances Louisa. She was eleven years old when she received this communication from her father.

Bushnell began with the reason for writing to his daughter. He told her:

> I have thought many times of the possibility that I may never see you again; in which case I should wish very much to have left you a father's message and counsel; and it is this, in part, which moves me to write to you now.[125]

He then proceeded to list his expectations of his daughters, expectations that never changed throughout his life. Bushnell noted, "I wish, in the best and truest sense, to have you become a woman."[126] However, he added, "I wish you to feel, as you grow up, that you are not doomed to any low or vain calling because you are a woman."[127] He told his daughter that becoming a woman would not be easy, and would require great and patient cultivation of every sort. Bushnell asserted that becoming a woman included the cultivation of character and mind (intelligence), a good knowledge of Latin, Greek, French, and German, and a perfectly pure heart like the heart of an infant.[128]

Bushnell's expectations of his daughters differed somewhat from "the cult of true womanhood" that arose in the nineteenth century. As mentioned in Chapter 1, Barbara Welter states that the attributes of True Womanhood were comprised of four cardinal virtues: piety [religion], purity, submissiveness, and domesticity.[129] If Bushnell's concept of true womanhood as stated in his letter is compared with Welter's theory, it becomes clear that Bushnell's communication to his daughter stressed the importance of purity and religion, but contained no mention of submissiveness and domesticity. Rather, he placed emphasis on the cultivation of character and intelligence, and a good knowledge of languages, along with religion and purity.

Whenever Bushnell used the term "Christian," it is important to understand that he actually meant "being religious." He noted:

> A woman should be a Christian. Her character should be the very blossom and flavor of piety. . . . Most men agree that a *woman* ought to be religious. . . . Therefore I am anxious, my dear daughter, that you should begin the Christian life now and grow up in it. . . . Be it, then, your first thought to be religious. Let your childhood be religious; your girlhood, and thus your womanhood,—your whole life, and thus your death and all beyond.[130]

Thus, when he spoke of his daughters and women as Christians, he was implying that they should be religious. In 1848 Bushnell again wrote to Frances Louisa, and advised her to turn to religion and God:

> I hope, [in the] meantime, that you will be turning your thoughts to religion and to God, as well as to your studies. . . . Unite yourself to Christ for life, and try to receive his beautiful and loving spirit. . . . We are a very happy family, and if we are all one together in Christ, it will secure our happiness in all future time.[131]

Bushnell repeatedly advised his daughters to be religious. When he used the term, "religion," he did not mean religion in the dogmatic sense, but referred to religion as a matter of practice. In his mind, religion had to do with the way in which one lived his or her life. He told his daughters, "Let your religious character come into the same good drill of practice, in the family, in the care of yourself, in society, in your works."[132] Therefore, it is also clear that Bushnell did not limit practical religion simply to family life, but also extended it to society.

Additionally, Bushnell expected his daughters to be charitable to the poor. A charitable spirit, in fact, seemed to be one of his more important expectations of women. In 1852, he wrote a letter to his

> I have made you out a long story, children, but you will see in it what rough things there are to be suffered by many poor people in this rough world. I hope that God will make you thankful for the sweet comforts crowded about you, and give you a heart to be as merciful as you ought to those who have none.[133]

The charitable spirit that he expected of his daughters led Bushnell to support women working as deaconesses in the church. Therefore, the concept of charity or benevolence was an important concept in his views of women.

In conclusion, Bushnell's attitude toward his daughters in family life was that of a nurturing father. Furthermore, he expected and encouraged his daughters to become women of character, as well as to be proficient in other languages, religious, and charitable. However, the one piece of advice that he did not give was that his daughters should be subordinate to men.

Summary of This Chapter

In this chapter, "Women in the Family," I have argued that Bushnell wished to form a solid marriage and family life on the ideal level by reinforcing men's patriarchal and hierarchical attitudes toward women. In this way, he hoped to build a strong foundation for a Christian America. In his own marriage and family life, however, Bushnell did not realize, nor did he even appear to attempt to realize his ideal. In this sense, his views of women in marriage and family life showed complexity between the ideal and the actual.

The Next Chapter

In the next chapter, "Women in the Church," I will argue that Bushnell wanted to entrust a strong church foundation to women, rather than to men. He believed that a strong foundation for the church would be accomplished especially through women's religious activities in the church. However, he rejected women's participation in the administrative works of the church. These attitudes also reveal the complexity of his thought with regard to women in the church.

Notes

1 Bushnell used the terms, "subordinate" and "subject" interchangeably. He sometimes referred to women's nature as "subject nature," and men's nature as "governing nature." Horace Bushnell, *Women's Suffrage; The Reform Against Nature* (New York: Charles Scribner and Company, 1869), 169.

2 Ibid., 52.

3 Ibid., 52.

4 Horace Bushnell, *Women's Suffrage; The Reform Against Nature,* 53.

5 Ibid., 170.

6 Ibid., 57.

7 A similar definition of the subordination of women can be found in Gerda Lerner's book, *The Creation of Patriarchy* (New York: Oxford University Press, 1986), 234. Lerner writes, "Subordination does not have the connotation of evil intent on the part of the dominant. . . . It includes the possibility of voluntary acceptance of subordinate status in exchange for protection and privilege, a condition which characterizes so much of the historical experience of women." I do not imply that Lerner accepts the notion of women's subordination. In fact, Lerner argues against such subordination.

8 Conservative pastors and theologians usually utilized the Bible to buttress their arguments. They expressed their understanding of women's nature to endorse and promote anti-suffrage sentiment. In 1837, "A Pastoral Letter of `the General Association of Massachusetts (Orthodox) to the Churches under Their Care" declared, "The appropriate duties and influence of woman are clearly stated in the New Testament. . . . But when she [woman] assumes the place and tone of man as a public reformer, our care and protection of her seem unnecessary." See Elizabeth Cady Stanton, Susan B. Anthony, and Matilda Joslyn Gage, eds., *History of Woman Suffrage* Vol. I (Rochester: Charles Mann, 1887), 81.

9 Bushnell, *Women's Suffrage; The Reform Against Nature,* 74. The word, "meet-helper," is Bushnell's.

10 Elizabeth Cady Stanton et al., *The Woman's Bible: Part I, Comments on Genesis, Exodus, Leviticus, Numbers and Deuteronomy* (New York: European Publishing Company, 1895), 14-22.

11 Stanton et al., 15-16.

12 Bushnell, *Women's Suffrage; The Reform Against Nature*, 76.

13 Ibid., 76.

14 Ibid., 76.

15 Ibid., 76-77.

16 Ibid., 77-78.

17 Stanton et al., *The Woman's Bible: Part I, Comments on Genesis, Exodus, Leviticus, Numbers and Deuteronomy*, 158.

18 Stanton et al., 159. Barbara Welter points out, "It is somewhat surprising, after all the vitriol directed against Paul, to see how small a part of the whole work [The Woman's Bible] is devoted to an analysis of his epistles." See Barbara Welter, "Something Remains to Dare: Introduction to *The Woman's Bible*," in *The Original Feminist Attack on the Bible*, by Elizabeth Cady Stanton et al. (Reprint, New York: Arno Press, 1974), xxiv.

19 Bushnell, *Women's Suffrage; The Reform Against Nature*, 79.

20 Ibid., 79.

21 Karen Halttunen, *Confidence Men and Painted Women: A Study of Middle-Class Culture in America, 1830-1870* (New Haven: Yale University Press, 1982), 64.

Halttunen also writes, "For the rising middle classes of the nineteenth century, fashion served both as a barrier which had to be surmounted by those entering the more privileged bourgeois circles and as a standard which could be applied to the claims of those seeking admission from below. . . . [M]iddle-class Americans strived to pass the fashion barrier by dressing stylishly and practicing ceremonial etiquette to a degree condemned by many [European] visitors as absurd." Ibid., 61-62.

In addition, she observes, "The life of fashion, in other words, undermined all moral self-improvement. Fashion was regarded as the art of surface illusion. . . .Young men and women of fashion were learning to cultivate a showy appearance at the expense of moral character." Ibid., 63.

22 Stanton et al., *The Woman's Bible: Part I, Comments on Genesis, Exodus, Leviticus, Numbers and Deuteronomy*, 174.

23 Bushnell, *Women's Suffrage; The Reform Against Nature*, 81.

24 Horace Bushnell, "The Age of Homespun," in *Work and Play* (New York: Charles Scribner, 1864), 383. This is a discourse which was delivered at the Centennial Celebration of Litchfield County, Connecticut, on August 14th, 1851.

25 Ibid., 383.

26 Susan Hill Lindley, *"You Have Stept Out Of Your Place": A History of Women and Religion in America* (Louisville: Westminster John Knox Press, 1996), 257-62.

27 Barbara Welter, "The Cult of True Womanhood: 1800-1860," in *Dimity Convictions: The American Woman in the Nineteenth Century* (Athens: Ohio University Press, 1976), 37, 209.

28 Carl N. Degler, *At Odds: Women and the Family in America from the Revolution to the Present* (New York: Oxford University Press, 1980), 152.

29 Bushnell, *Women's Suffrage; The Reform Against Nature*, 153. Michael G. Lawler acknowledges Paul Palmer's clarification of the difference between covenant and contract. Lawler cites Palmer: "Contracts are made for a stipulated period of time; covenants are forever. Contracts can be broken . . . covenants cannot be broken, but if violated, they result in personal loss and broken hearts." In addition, Lawler remarks, "The image of marriage as covenant has been traditionally a Protestant approach; the Catholic tradition has imaged it as sacrament." See Michael G. Lawler, "Sacrament of Marriage," in *The New Dictionary of Sacramental Worship*, 1990.

30 Bushnell, *Women's Suffrage; The Reform Against Nature*, 153-54.

31 Bushnell, "The Age of Homespun," 385.

32 See also Bushnell's "Acknowledgment" in *Women's Suffrage; The Reform Against Nature*. Bushnell noted of his own wife: "She has been with me in many weaknesses and some storms, giving strength alike in both." Bushnell, *Women's Suffrage; The Reform Against Nature*, no pagination.

33 Horace Bushnell, *Christian Nurture* (New York: Charles Scribner, 1861; reprint, Grand Rapids: Baker Book House, 1979), 195. Throughout Bushnell's works, the notion of polygamy was mentioned only here.

34 Horton Davies, "Congregationalist," in *A New Dictionary of Liturgy & Worship*, 1986.

35 Ibid., 355.

36 Horace Bushnell, "A Marriage Ceremony," in *The Spirit in Man*, ed. Mary Bushnell Cheney (New York: Charles Scribner's Sons, 1903), 385-87. According to his commemorative discourse for the twentieth anniversary of the North Congregational Church, Bushnell united 168 couples in marriage during the period from 1833 until 1853. He noted: "During the twenty years now past there have been added to the church by profession, 435; by letter, 356; in all 791. I have baptized 249 infants, and probably about 200 adults. I have united 168 couples in marriage. The number of funerals I have attended I do not exactly know—probably between 250 and 300." See Horace Bushnell, *A Commemorative Discourse* (Hartford: Elihu Geer, 1853), 11-12.

37 Bushnell, "A Marriage Ceremony," 386.

38 Ibid., 386.

39 David G. Hackett, "Gender and Religion in American Culture, 1870-1930," *Religion and American Culture* 5, no. 2 (Summer 1995): 133.

40 Ronald William Hogeland, "Femininity and the Nineteenth Century Post-Puritan Mind" (Ph.D. diss., University of California, Loa Angeles, 1968), 173.

41 Kathryn Kish Sklar presents a complex view about the roles of men and women in Bushnell's Christian Nurture based on his "American Politics" and *Christian Nurture*: "Although Bushnell did not exclude fathers from nuturing responsibilities, he obviously expected them to bridge both the domestic and outside worlds, while mothers were to dwell only in 'a place of quiet' and have 'quiet minds which the din of our public war never embroils'." See Kathryn Kish Sklar, *Catharine Beecher: A Study in American Domesticity* (New York: W.W. Norton & Company, Inc., 1976), 309.

42 Mary P. Ryan, *The Empire of the Mother: American Writing about Domesticity, 1830-1860* (New York: The Institute for Research in History and The Haworth Press, 1982), 8.

43 Nancy F. Cott, "On Men's History and Women's History," in *Meanings for Manhood: Construction of Masculinity in Victorian America*, ed. Mark C. Carnes and Clyde Griffen (Chicago and London: The University of Chicago Press, 1990), 207-08.

44 Colleen McDannell, *The Christian Home in Victorian America, 1840-1900* (Bloomington: Indiana University Press, 1986), 108-09.

45 Ibid., 127.

46 E. Anthony Rotundo, *American Manhood: Transformation in Masculinity from the Revolution to the Modern Era* (New York: BasicBooks, 1993).

Gail Bederman also makes an interesting observation in her work, *Manliness & Civilizaton: A Cultural History of Gender and Race in the United States*, 1880-1917 (Chicago: The University of Chicago Press, 1995), 17-18:

> "Although historians usually use the terms 'manly' and 'masculine' interchangeably, as if they were synonymous, the two words carried quite different connotations throughout the nineteenth century. Until about 1890, literate Victorians rarely referred to individual men as 'masculine.' Instead, admirable men were called 'manly.' After 1890, however, the words 'masculine' and 'masculinity' began to be used far more frequently—precisely because they could convey the new attributes of powerful manhood which middle-class men were working to synthesize."

I have found that Bushnell used the term, "manly," much more often than the term, "masculine." However, when he used the term, "manly," he sometimes combined that term with "women." For instance, he did not like "manly women."

47 Rotundo, 10. Of course, the two other institutions of society—church and state—were also governed only by men. Ibid., 11.

48 Ibid., 12.

49 Ibid., 12.

50 Ibid., 11-12.

51 Ibid., 12.

52 Ibid., 12-13. The term, "organic" is Rotundo's.

53 Ibid., 3. Michael Kimmel points out that "the term *self-made man* was an American neologism, first coined by Henry Clay in a speech in the U.S. Senate in 1832." See Michael Kimmel, *Manhood in America: A Cultural History* (New York: The Free Press, 1996), 26.

54 Rotundo, 3.

55 Ibid., 3.

56 Ibid.., 4, 19. Although Michael Kimmel calls this second phase the cult of the Self-Made Man, his definition of the Self-Made Man is similar to that of Rotundo's self-made manhood. Kimmel notes, "In the growing commercial[,] and soon, industrial society of the newly independent America, the Self-Made Man seemed to be born at the same time as his country." He further writes that the proving ground of being self-made was the public sphere, specifically the workplace; and that the workplace was considered to be a man's world. See Kimmel, 17, 26.

57 Rotundo,28.

58 Ibid., 5-6.

59 Of course, John M. Mulder does not forget to comment, "the special role of mothers in shaping the spiritual lives of their children formed an important theme of his book and evangelical Protestantism during the nineteenth century." John M. Mulder, "Introduction," in *Christian Nurture*, by Horace Bushnell (Reprint, Grand Rapids: Baker Book House, 1979), *xxix-xxx*.

60 Jerry W. McCant, "Nurture Is Not the Problem," *Christian Education Journal* 5, no. 2 (1984): 57.

61 Ibid., 66.

62 Ibidl, 59.

63 Mark Edwards, "'My God and My Good Mother': The Irony of Horace Bushnell's Gendered Republic," *Religion and American Culture: A Journal of Interpretation* 13, no. 1 (2003): 120.

64 Bushnell, *Christian Nurture*, 399.

65 Ibid., 236-37.

66 Ibid., 366. Bushnell, furthermore, remarked, "Timothy was supposed to have a complete set of recollections from his mother woven into his very feeling of the truth itself. It was more true because it had been taught him by her. There was even a sense of her loving personality in it, by which it always had been, and was always to be, endeared." Ibid., 370.

67 Bushnell, *Christian Nurture*, 397.

68 Ibid., 397.

69 Ibid., 398.

70 McDannell, 112.

71 Bushnell, *Christian Nurture*, 315.

72 Ibid., 315.

73 Ibid., 315.

74 Ibid.,, 317.

75 Ibid., 317.

76 Ibid., 333.

77 Ibid., 344-45.

78 Ibid., 250.

79 Ibid., 257.

80 Ibid., 257-58.

81 Ibid., 301.

82 Ibid., 303-04.

83 Horace Bushnell, "God's Way with a Soul," in *Life and Letters of Horace Bushnell*, ed. Mary Bushnell Cheney (New York: Harper & Brothers, Publishers, 1880; reprint, New York: Arno Press & *The New York Times*, 1969), 1-2. This is a fragment of Horace Bushnell's autobiography which was dimly pencilled on a stray sheet of paper.

84 Horace Bushnell, "Sketches of His Grandmother and Mother," in *Life and Letters of Horace Bushnell*, ed. Mary Bushnell Cheney (New York: Harper & Brothers, Publishers, 1880; reprint, New York: Arno Press & *The New York Times*, 1969), 24-34.

85 Bushnell, "Sketches of His Grandmother and Mother," 26-27.

86 See Chapters 3 and 4.

87 Bushnell, "God's Way with a Soul," 1-2.

88 Bushnell, "Sketches of His Grandmother and Mother," 29. The term, maternal sacrifice, is Bushnell's.

89 This point will be further discussed in detail in Chapter 3.

90 Bushnell, "Sketches of His Grandmother and Mother," 29, 31-32.

91 Ibid., 32.

92 Bushnell, "Sketches of His Grandmother and Mother," 27.

93 This will be discussed in detail in Chapter 4.

94 Mary Bushnell Cheney, ed., *Life and Letters of Horace Bushnell* (New York: Harper & Brothers, Publishers, 1880; reprint, New York: Arno Press & *The New York Times*, 1969), 462.

95 Ibid., 7.

96 Hogeland, 175.

97 Robert L. Edwards, *Of Singular Genius, Of Singular Grace: A Biography of Horace Bushnell* (Cleveland: The Pilgrim Press, 1992), 3.

98 Ibid., 66.

99 Cheney, ed., 90.

100 Ibid., 113-14.

101 Ibid., 354.

102 Ibid., 352-53.

103 Ibid., 89.

104 Bushnell, *Women's Suffrage; The Reform Against Nature*, 71-72.

105 Cheney, ed., 102.

106 Ibid., 103.

107 Bushnell, *Christian Nurture*, 406.

108 Cheney, ed., 111.

109 Ibid., 111.

110 To Bushnell, the concept of an angel was important not only in his views of women but also in his views of Christianity. When he confessed his faith in 1822, he said, "In the presence of God and angels and men, I vowed to be the Lord's, in an everlasting covenant never to be broken." Ibid., 21. In addition, in his 1843 response to Mrs. S. [Bushnell's parishioner], he regarded angels as "the ministers and missionaries of Christ." Ibid., 101. Allison Coudert mentions, "Christian angels are God's messengers and ministers. . . . Angels are actively involved in the daily lives of Christians." Allison Coudert, "Angels," in *The Encyclopedia of Religion* vol. 1, 1987.

111 Cheney, ed., 275.

112 Ibid., 275.

113 A detailed discussion regarding Bushnell's views of minister's wife can be found in Chapter 3, "Women in the Church."

114 The phrase, "the Christly spirit" is Bushnell's. Cheney, ed., 446.

115 Cheney, ed., 277.

116 Ibid., 349.

117 Ibid., 191-92. Edwards, *Of Singular Genius, Of Singular Grace*, 96.

118 Cheney, ed., 192.

119 Ibid., 191. Edwards, *Of Singular Genius, Of Singular Grace*, 96.

120 Edwards, *Of Singular Genius, Of Singular Grace*, 97. Cheney, ed., 191. Robert Bruce Mullin, *The Puritan as Yankee* (Grand Rapids: William S. Eerdmans Publishing Company, 2002), 128-30.

121 Bushnell, *Women's Suffrage; The Reform Against Nature*, 183.

122 Mullin, 246.

123 Cheney, ed., 429.

124 Ibid., 428-29.

125 Cheney, ed., 139. This is a letter written on October 6, 1845, at Geneva, Switzerland.

126 Ibid., 140.

127 Ibid., 140.

128 In his first letter to his daughter in New Haven, Bushnell wrote on July 23, 1843, "My dear child, you are growing up into a woman very fast. I have a great desire that you should endeavor to make yourself the best and loveliest of women, to have a wise character, a gentle heart, pure and simple manners, and, in a word, be such that everybody will be your friend." Ibid., 108-09.

129 Welter, "The Cult of True Womanhood: 1800-1860," 21.

130 Cheney, ed., 142-43.

131 Ibid., 189. As Robert L. Edwards mentions, the Bushnells were quite a happy family, "unlike the Henry Ward Beechers, whose domestic life was difficult." Therefore, reflecting on his own family life, Bushnell linked the happiness of the family with the religiosity of the women. Edwards, *Of Singular Genius, Of Singular Grace*, 217.

132 Cheney, ed., 434.

133 Ibid., 273.

CHAPTER 3
WOMEN IN THE CHURCH

Religious Natures of Women and Men

The Difference Between Male and Female Religious Natures

Horace Bushnell distinguished his views on the religious natures of women and men from his views on the general natures of women and men,—although, from his perspective, both natures were closely related. As mentioned in Chapter 2, Bushnell understood that women's nature should be subordinate to men and that it should be integral to men's nature to govern women. But he also noted:

> There is an aspect of privilege, in this matter of subordination, which, instead of inferring the inferiority of women, gives them, when morally [religiously] considered, the truest and sublimest conditions of ascendency. The highest virtues, purest in motive and really most difficult, are never to be looked for in the most forward and potentially regnant states. They belong rather to the subject conditions, where the coarse admixtures of pride and worldly power are shut away.[1]

In this way, Bushnell thought women would be stronger in virtues and purer in motive than men. That is, he understood women's religious nature as superior to men's. On the other hand, he believed that men should be sovereign and seek "pride and worldly power."

In addition, Bushnell commented:

> Their moral nature [Women's religious nature] is more delicately perceptive. Their religious inspirations, or inspirabilities, put them closer to God, as having a more celestial property and affinities more superlative. . . .

> [Woman's brain is] capable . . . of a more delicately [delicate] feeling and bright insight.[2]

Bushnell believed that the striking characteristics of women's religious nature were their perceptivity, inspiration, feeling, and bright insight. He also believed that women's religious nature was "closer to God" than men's because theirs had a more heaven-like quality.

Metaphors of the Law and the Gospel

Bushnell elucidated the above description of male and female religious natures by using the metaphors of the Law and the Gospel. In other words, he compared the religious nature of men to the metaphor of the Law, and that of women to the metaphor of the Gospel.[3]

With regard to men's religious nature, Bushnell offered the following illustration:

> The law, which is the man, goes before [the Gospel or the woman], rough-hewing the work of government. It is Sinai-like, and speaks in thunder. It commands, and, by sanctions of force, where force is wanted, vindicates its own supreme authority. It so far has priority in rule, that it never can have any thing less; for the cessation of law is the cessation of government, and if it should only fall into second place or equal place with any thing else, it would lose the inherent sovereignty of its nature, when it can be law no longer.[4]

Therefore, the law (the man) functioned as government, commanded the Gospel (the woman), and used force as an expression of its (his) authority.

As regards the religious nature of women, Bushnell turned to the Gospel:

> The gospel coming after [the Law] in order is the woman. It is subject as gospel to the husband, that is, to the law; it is made under the law; and the whole historic operation, by which it is organized, is itself obedience, submission, love, and sacrifice. And it is so perfectly subject to the law, that it professes nothing but a fulfillment of the law, and a universal recovery to it.[5]

Hence, Bushnell thought that the Gospel (the woman) was created under the Law (the man), was subject to it, and embodied the qualities of obedience, submission, love, and sacrifice.

In short, the Gospel (a metaphor for the religious nature of women) was created after the Law (a metaphor for the religious nature of men) and was subject to the Law in order to fulfill the Law. The function of the Law was government or rule, while the function of the Gospel was obedience, submission, love, and sacrifice.

However, at the same time, Bushnell believed that the Gospel was superior to the Law. He wrote:

> Which of these [the Law and the Gospel] is superior? . . . Undoubtedly it is the gospel. It goes above the law in doing every thing for it, and overtops it in glory, by submission to it. No power is in it, but the power of suffering and a subject state. It lives in sorrow and dies in sacrifice, and accomplishes just what the law could not accomplish. The coarse ideas of force, and majesty, and all the pomps and thunders of enforcement are omitted here, and the simple wifehood of God's love, and beauty, is revealed, by what is lowliest and most dejected. And this is grace, the world-transforming grace in which God's empire culminates.[6]

So, although the Gospel had no power in itself, it possessed the power of sorrow, suffering, sacrifice, love and beauty in its submission to the Law.

Through the use of this metaphor, Bushnell built an argument for the transformative power of women's religious nature. He declared that women's religious nature (a nature that is found in the power of sorrow, suffering, sacrifice, love and beauty in submission to men), rather than their political power, would transform the world into God's Kingdom. Bushnell wanted America to become God's empire in the future. God's empire, however, had to be supported by women's religious contributions, rather than by their political contributions.

Therefore, Bushnell was indeed frustrated by the women of his era who wanted to acquire political power. He stated:

> "Give us power," they say; and power to them is force, or an equal right of command. . . . Here is their true power, in a disinterested and subject life of good. And there is a way in this to govern men, that is greatness itself and victory . . . . When if she [woman] could only consent to be true gospel and woman together, to be gentle, and patient, and right, and fearless, how certainly would she come out superior and put him at her feet.

> There seems to me, in this view, I confess, to be something sacred, or angelic, in such womanhood.[7]

Thus, he did not endorse women who desired political power. Instead, he entreated them to realize their general nature of subordination and their religious nature rooted in sorrow, suffering, sacrifice, love and beauty. Furthermore, Bushnell asserted that if women were faithful to both their general and religious natures, then they could eventually manipulate men. However, it is interesting to note that he did not seem to offer specific and concrete ways for women to reach the goals he laid before them. Rather, his suggestion remained abstract.

Even though Bushnell's writings did not specifically name any of the leaders of the women's suffrage movement, it is clear that he was arguing against leaders such as Elizabeth Cady Stanton, Susan B. Anthony, Matilda Joslyn Gage, Isabella Beecher Hooker, John Hooker, Henry Ward Beecher, William Lloyd Garrison, Francis Ellen Burr, and others.

Religious Nature of Women and Bushnell's Idea of God

Bushnell's views of the religious natures of women and men were related to his idea of God revealed in Jesus Christ. He had himself experienced God as his personal "friend" in 1848-1849.[8] In a letter to his wife from Savannah [Cuba] in 1855, he wrote:

> We should most naturally expect that God would not hide himself from his creatures. He loves them, invites their love to him, asks them to be in terms of friendship with him. And what is this but to say that he will hear, communicate, be open to and receive their desires, doing for and with them as friends do, because they are friends.[9]

He also noted the importance of the aspects of God's beautiful feeling and character, and God's friendly and attractive being in *Christian Nurture*.[10]

The above citations suggest that Bushnell viewed God and Jesus Christ not as fearful beings, but as loving, friendly, and tender persons. This image of a loving, friendly, and tender God and Christ was linked to love and vicarious sacrifice, qualities that were the core of women's religious nature. In contrast, men's religious nature basically reflected none of these qualities.

Themes of Love and Vicarious Sacrifice: Bushnell and Stanton

The themes of love and vicarious sacrifice appear in various works by Bushnell.[11] In *Nature and the Supernatural, as together Constituting the One System of God*, he noted, "There is a vicarious spirit in love; all love inserts itself vicariously into the sufferings and woes and, in a certain sense, the sins of others, taking them on itself as a burden."[12]

In *The Vicarious Sacrifice, Grounded in Principles of Universal Obligation*, he explained, "Love is a principle essentially vicarious in its own nature, identifying the subject with others, so as to suffer their adversities and pains, and taking on itself the burden of their evils."[13] He also noted:

> Love itself is an essentially vicarious principle. . . . See how it is with love in the case of a mother. She loves her child, and it comes out in that fact, or from it, that she watches for the child, bears all its pains and sickness on her own feeling, and when it is wronged, is stung herself, by the wrong put upon it, more bitterly far than the child. She takes every chance of sacrifice for it, as her own opportunity.[14]

Furthermore, Bushnell indicated that God's love is fully revealed in Jesus Christ through vicarious sacrifice.[15]

In *Forgiveness and Law, Grounded in Principles*, he remarked, "All love, as we perceive, reveals the vicarious instinct, either natural or religious. . . . The mother, the friend, the patriot, are all specially charged with their own special burden of concern or sorrow."[16] Thus, certain people (such as mothers, friends, and patriots) were able to embody the qualities of vicarious sacrifice and the like in given circumstances.

Interestingly, Bushnell's last letter, written to his wife on August 10, 1874, was about the connection between love and sacrifice. He told her:

> What can ever make up the Gospel we want but to have the love coming in the line of a forgiveness? It really does not come to be a salvation till the love is seen making cost, and coming after as by sacrifice. It would not be difficult for even a heathen to believe in God as love; but to believe that he comes after us through painstaking and sorrow would be very far off,—ah, it is impossible![17]

In *Life and Letters of Horace Bushnell,* his daughter, Frances Louisa Bushnell, offered a summary of her father's theological correlation between love and self-sacrifice:

> The central idea of the book [*The Vicarious Sacrifice*], that on which all its arguments turn, is *the self-sacrifice of God in Christ.* In the very title of his first book, *God in Christ,* he had struck the keynote; but now he heard the music of a fuller harmony. That idea had become to him the centre of the universe, and in its own nature a reconciler.[18]

Elizabeth Cady Stanton, one of Bushnell's contemporaries and a leader of the women's suffrage movement in nineteenth-century America took a different view of the matter. She decidedly rejected the concept of self-sacrifice as being the core of women's religious nature. Stanton declared:

> So a woman, who spends all her time in churches, with priests, in charities, neglects to cultivate her own natural gifts, to make the most of herself as an individual in the scale of being, a responsible soul whose place no other can fill, is worse than an infidel. "Self-development is a higher duty than self-sacrifice," should be woman's motto henceforward.[19]

Stanton, therefore, believed that a woman's highest duty was to herself and her personal development as an individual. Bushnell's idea of self-sacrifice, then, was in sharp contrast with Stanton's concept of self-development.

Two Different Marys: The Mother of Jesus and The Woman Who Anointed Jesus

To support his argument in favor of women's superiority in terms of their religious nature, and to support the contention that women were not inferior to men in their general nature, Bushnell cited two different Marys: the mother of Jesus and the woman who anointed Jesus in the New Testament. He regarded Mary, the mother of Jesus, as an ideal woman in terms of women's religious and general natures.[20] In his book, *Women's Suffrage; The Reform Against Nature,* Bushnell emphasized that Mary's subordination to Joseph did not make her inferior to him.[21] Thus, by using her as an example, Bushnell supported and confirmed the notion that subordination, in terms of women's nature, did not imply inferiority.

Bushnell's sermon, "Mary, the Mother of Jesus" clearly shows the connection between Mary and women's religious nature. He repeatedly preached this sermon, reading it first to a small circle of friends at Edwin E. Parker's house, and later preaching it at South Church, Park Church, and Asylum Hill Church in Hartford.[22] This was also the last sermon that Bushnell publicly delivered.[23] In the sermon, he stated:

> [Mary] has read the prophets too, as we may judge, and her feeling, like all the religious feeling of her nation, is leavened in this manner, by indefinite yearning for the coming of that wonderful unknown being called Messiah. And so her opening womanly nature has been stretching itself Messiahward, and configuring itself inwardly to what the unknown Great One is to be.[24]

First, Bushnell portrayed Mary as a woman who lived her life in the hope of the Messiah. Then, he linked her "womanly nature" to her earnest desire to stretch Messiahward. That is, Bushnell suggested that a true womanly nature began with a yearning for the Messiah. This crucial point is characteristic of Bushnell: without religious meaning, the natures of man and woman cannot be realized.

Bushnell referred to Mary as "divine motherhood before the worlds,"[25] "true motherhood,"[26] and "royal motherhood."[27] It is significant that he used the words, "divine," "true," and "royal" before the word "motherhood" when describing Mary. Thus, he identified Mary as the model of the ideal woman and mother.

Bushnell also paid attention to the silence and stillness of Mary. This may be because he was nervous about the noisiness of women, the home, the world, and others. Bushnell seemed to long for quiet. He contrasted the aspects of Mary's silence and stillness to the behaviors of the other people who followed Jesus. He wrote:

> On the way out a great company of people follow, comprising many women who go to bewail him [Jesus], and make up the procession of mourners. Mary, the mother, was deep enough in mourning, but she could not join that noisy company, and it does not appear that the other two Marys, Magdalene and the wife of Cleopas, were in it. . . . She does not toss her arms in shrieks and wild hysteric wailings.[28]

In the above citation, Bushnell seemed implicitly to slander the women who supported women's suffrage and whose campaign groups, in his view, were noisy and hysterical. He summed up Mary's silence and stillness with another beautiful word picture, "About all we can say of her [Mary], therefore, under her embargo of silence, is that she appears until she disappears; which she does—most wonderful, most nearly divine of all human characters—in the stillness of a snow-flake falling into the sea."[29] Bushnell continued his praise by adding:

> That grace of bearing, that sweet, devout modesty, such as became the motherhood of everlasting innocence. . . . Her unspotted motherhood, what can ye show of silent flowering in the white of purity, which she does not much better show herself![30]

Not only was Mary the embodiment of silence and stillness, but she also was spotless and pure, devout, and modest. Thus, in Bushnell's mind, Mary's qualities became the qualities to which all mothers should aspire.

In addition to Mary, the mother of Jesus, Bushnell was favorable to the Mary who anointed Jesus. He called her "a simple-hearted loving woman."[31] The reason Bushnell liked this Mary was that, in his view, she consistently had the delicate perception, inspiration, feeling, and bright insight that he considered to be characteristics of women's religious nature. Mary also embodied the love and vicarious sacrifice that he saw as the core of women's religious nature.

In his essay, "The Insight of Love," Bushnell reflected on Mary's deep spirituality:

> By a certain delicate affinity of feeling that was equal to insight, and almost to prophecy, she touches exactly her Lord's strange, unknown future, and anoints him for the kingdom and the death she does not even think of, or know. Plainly enough no debate of consequences could ever have prepared her for these deep and beautifully wise proprieties.[32]

In addition, this passage included an implicit critique of the "debate" that suffragists utilized as their strategy in order to get into the political world.

Bushnell also commented on Mary's embodiment of love and vicarious sacrifice. He follows:

> She does not love him [Jesus] on debate, or serve him by contrived reasons, but she is so drunk up in his person, so totally captivated by the wondrous something felt in him, that she has and can have no thought other than to love him, and do every thing out of her love.[33]

Here again, Bushnell was implicitly criticizing the women who wanted to enter the political world through the means of argument and discussion in favor of female suffrage. He also was criticizing women who neglected their religious natures of bright insight and spontaneously sacrificial love.

In his concluding remarks found in the sermon, "The Insight of Love," Bushnell praised the woman who anointed Jesus:

> All acts of beauty and good are like that of the woman, coming to anoint her Lord—inspirations of the beauty she loved, wise without study or contrivance, unconscious, spontaneous, and free. This now is society, this is character; to this height of perfection, this blessedness in good, our God is raising all that love him.[34]

To Bushnell, the two Marys—the mother of Jesus and the woman who anointed Jesus—were individuals who represented his notion of women's religious nature. Jesus' mother, Mary, was a silent, still, and pure woman. The woman who anointed Jesus had the insight of who Jesus was and loved him for it. Based on these two illustrations, it is clear that Bushnell wanted women to remain within their religious nature. It is also clear that he was criticizing females who were ardently involved with women's suffrage and who utilized aggressive debate and reason to accomplish their goal. Thus, the two Marys had significant meaning to Bushnell not only in the religious sense, but also as tools for discouraging women from entering the world of politics.

Women's Roles in Church

Bushnell and Women's Roles in the Church

Bushnell placed a high value on women's religious nature. He believed that it contributed to a solid church, which to him was a crucial institution for realizing a Christian America. My argument in this section is that Bushnell was much more open to women's roles in the church than has been previously thought. That is, he was open provided that men's government of women and women's subordination to men were retained within the church. In order to understand Bushnell's approach to the subject, it is helpful to investigate the various ways in which nineteenth-century American women participated in the activities of the church.

Lindley's Three Models of Women's Ministry

Susan Hill Lindley discerns three models of women's religious leadership (women's ministry) in nineteenth-century America. The first is the preaching model. Lindley notes that women preachers and their acceptance was important, not only because it laid the essential groundwork for female ordination, but also because female preaching itself was a significant issue in the nineteenth century.[35] Phoebe Palmer (1807-1874) is the best representative of this model of women's ministry. Despite Palmer's success as a preacher, Lindley observes that she was not an advocate of female ordination, women's sacramental ministry, or other women's rights issues.[36] Palmer's attitude implies that the preaching model of women's ministry did not necessarily pave the way for women's ordination, nor did it automatically lead to the women's rights movement. In fact, Lindley explains that Palmer "accepted and valued the domestic role of wife and mother as natural and divinely sanctioned for women, subordinate only to every believer's first duty to God."[37]

The second model of women's ministry is the ordination model. The ordination of women was a highly contested idea. Those women who dared to pursue this role encountered strong opposition, and sometimes the pressure was too much to bear. For example, Antoinette Brown (1825-1921) was invited in 1853 to the First Congregational Church in Butler, New York to serve as its pastor. In the same year, she was formally ordained as the first woman minister in America, but resigned her position in 1854. The reasons for her resignation included, according to Lindley, the fact that she was pulled between the majority of Christians, who opposed women's preaching and ordination, and her friends in the women's rights movement like Lucy Stone, Elizabeth Cady Stanton, and Susan B. Anthony, who were critical of the Bible and the organized church.[38]

The third model of ministry is the deaconess model. A deaconess was a religious woman, who served people in need. According to Lindley, the deaconess movement in the second half of the nineteenth century offered women yet another model of ministry.[39] The first attempt to establish a female diaconate in America was made by the Lutheran denomination. The Institution of Protestant Deaconesses, the first organization for deaconesses in America was formed in

1850.[40] Lindley, however, adds that the deaconess movement "achieved its greatest visibility and participation" within Methodism. She credits Lucy Rider Meyer (1849-1922), founder of the Chicago Training School, with much of the movement's success within Methodism.[41]

Lindley's three models of women's ministry in nineteenth-century America are helpful in investigating Bushnell's views regarding women's ministry. As will be discussed later in this section, Bushnell supported women's preaching and women as deaconesses, but rejected women's ordination.

Zikmund's Analysis of Women Preachers

With regard to women preachers, Barbara Brown Zikmund analyzes basic nineteenth-century arguments for and against the issue in America.[42] She notes that the most pervasive and simplest argument in favor of women preachers was the emphasis on a call from the Lord through the work of the Holy Spirit. She also states that another argument was based in pragmatism, since these women were regarded as effective in advancing ministry. Zikmund adds that because women were already engaged in ministry, they needed to be recognized as preachers. Furthermore, she says that arguments in favor of female preachers were strengthened by the reinterpretation of the Bible as it related to women. The most radical form of this reinterpretation was the *Woman's Bible* published in 1895 and 1898 under the leadership of Elizabeth Cady Stanton.

Zikmund observes that, on the other side of the issue, one argument against preaching women was based on biblical authority. She writes that another argument claimed men and women were not equal regarding rule and authority, although they were equal in their respective spheres. She notes, furthermore, that other arguments were based on social, historical, and political reasons, such as women's role as mothers or the rejection of the foundational idea of the women's rights movement.[43]

Although Zikmund did not necessarily cover women's ordination and deaconesses, her classification of the arguments for and against preaching women is helpful for an understanding of Bushnell's views on women's preaching in the church. Utilizing Zikmund's analysis, it is then clear that Bushnell supported women's preaching because he believed that women were pragmatically effective in advancing ministry.

Olson's Analysis

To analyze Bushnell's views, it is also necessary to have some background on the deaconess movement. Jeannine E. Olson notes that although deacons and deaconesses had many roles that varied with time and place, their roles could be placed under two broad categories: liturgy and charity.[44] She also points out that the deaconess movement in America began among Lutherans, but grew with amazing speed in the nineteenth century within the Methodist denomination.[45] In addition, her study conveys that the work of deaconesses was rather low among nineteenth-century Congregationalists.[46] Bushnell was a Congregationalist pastor; however, despite the low interest of his denomination, he acknowledged the importance of deaconess work.

Women's Higher Participation in Work of the Church

Bushnell understood that women were more involved in church work than men. He stated, "The womanly nature, being a subject nature, is specially flexible and free to the Christian inspirations, and for this reason, doubtless, it is that more than twice as many women as men are engaged in Christian work and relations."[47] In addition, he noted that women had more insight about Christian truth than men; women's piety ranged higher than that of men; women prayed more than men; and women did more volunteer work than men.[48] Thus, he connected and explicated the reason behind women's higher participation in Christian work with that of men based on the differing religious natures of men and women.

Bushnell's Views on Women's Public Speaking in the Church

Women's public speaking in the church was one of the controversial religious issues in nineteenth-century America. Bushnell did not oppose women who publicly addressed the congregation, as long as they did not try to obtain access and rights to administrative roles in the church, and as long as they did not lose the womanliness of their voices and physical appearance.

Bushnell wrote:

> As regards the ministry of the word, or the matter of public speaking in the churches, it is very evident what Paul lays down as restriction in the 11th and 14th chapters of his *First Epistle to the Corinthians*— requiring in the former that no woman pray or prophesy with her head uncovered, and in the latter that she keep silence altogether—that all such restriction is now gone by.[49]

Bushnell went on to give his interpretation of the eleventh and fourteenth chapters of Paul's First Epistle to the Corinthians:

> The "speaking" here . . . appears to be not exactly prophesying and praying in the Spirit, but a speaking as in council and authority—a debating of administrative matters, where they will put themselves in measure with men, and assume a power of leadership which does not belong to them—is plainly meant to be included.[50]

Thus, Bushnell did not accept women's church governance. He explained, "When we come to matters of church administration and presiding rule, these do not come within their [women's] jurisdiction. They can not, in true Christian order, be made pastors, or presbyters, or bishops; no one of the apostles ever heard of such a thing."[51]

The above citations clearly show that Bushnell did not deny women's public speaking in the church, but was opposed to women taking on governing functions. In other words, as long as women did not pursue any form of church government, he thought that it was permissible for women to preach to the congregation.

He believed that "the question of ministration was one thing, and the question of administration another."[52] It seems appropriate that, with reference to women's ministry, Bushnell should conclude: "As regards women's clerical profession, only it is clear as need be that a much larger and more forward operation is permissible, without damage to the Christian order, and with real advantage to the Christian cause."[53]

Furthermore, he explained, "When we ask how far the clerical profession is open, or may be, to women, there is no objection to allowing that anything which belongs to the quickening, and edifying of assemblies in the Spirit may be left open to them."[54] Utilizing Zikmund's classification of the arguments for preaching women then, Bushnell may be classified as someone who supported them for their pragmatic effectiveness in advancing ministry.

Bushnell also supported women's speaking in the church based on the following evidence:

> Nobody has ever observed that Lucretia Mott, or any speaker of the Quaker sisterhood, long practiced in the prophesying of the Spirit, has been hardening in voice, or look, or becoming in any respect less womanly. . . . The right of speaking for religion, under the inspirations of religion, belongs apparently to women as to men. And if

> women have gifts that qualify them specially for such ministrations, there appears to be no good reason longer why they should be kept under the ban of silence.[55]

He was, therefore, convinced that female preaching was acceptable because women like Lucretia Mott, who had long been accustomed to preaching, did not lose their feminine qualities. One of Bushnell's major concerns was the physical appearance and behavior of women. He was afraid that female physical appearance and behavior would resemble that of men if they became involved in the administrative matters of the church and if they participated in the women's suffrage movement. This is another reason Bushnell denied women access to church administration and leadership, although he was open to women preaching and a deaconess work.

Bushnell's Awareness of the Importance of Deaconess Work

Bushnell believed that it was proper for a woman to assume a deaconess role and to attend to public service as a mission. Although he himself was not involved in the deaconess movement, Bushnell supported parishioner Mary Lyman Collins' work in hospitals and with the poor, as will be explained later in this chapter. He also urged his own daughters to be charitable to the poor, as noted in Chapter 2. In addition, he made mention of the women found in the last chapter of Paul's Epistle to the Romans: Pheobe, Priscilla, Mary, Junia, Persis, and Rufus' mother. Bushnell highly valued the service of these biblical women, and considered their work to be almost equal to the ministry of the apostle Paul.[56]

As mentioned previously, Olson points out that the roles of deacons and deaconesses could be placed under two broad categories: liturgy and charity. By applying Olson's categories to Bushnell, one can see that he did not perceive liturgy to be the role of deacons and deaconesses, but was comfortable with their role in the area of charity. In addition, Olson suggests that among the Congregationalists, the work of the deaconess and the interest in her work were rather low in the nineteenth century. And yet, despite this tendency within his denomination, Bushnell was very aware of the importance of deaconess work and supported women's forays into the deaconate.

Bushnell's Disagreement with Women's Suffrage

Turning to the women of his era, especially the women of New England, Bushnell was disturbed that females were trying to obtain political power, rather than dedicating themselves to religious matters in the church. Clearly frustrated by the women's suffrage movement, he wrote:

> The call is now for women to buckle on the harness of political life and challenge the right to fight common battles with men. The subject nature is now to be adjourned, and the self-willed, governing nature to take its place; and the result will be, of course, that only half as many women will accept the cross, because they too are learning now to fight out their will; and the count of Christian men will also be reduced, because the number that have Christian wives who have grace to win their husbands is reduced. The result of course will be, if this reform [women's suffrage] is carried, that the number of them that believe will be greatly diminished, and whole centuries of toilsome progress will be lost, as it were, in a day.[57]

One of the reasons for his disagreement with women's suffrage is that he believed it would disturb the Christianization of America, a goal for which male ministers had labored for a century. In other words, Bushnell was worried about the numerical decline of Christians. Some Christian wives, who brought their husbands into the church, were beginning to be interested in political matters, such as women's suffrage. From Bushnell's perspective, women's suffrage would weaken the foundation of the church because it would divert women's attention from religious matters. Thus, the church, one of the crucial institutions for building a Christian America, would suffer—-as would the process of overall Christianization.

In addition, Bushnell thought that women themselves would suffer personally:

> And yet the bitterest, heaviest part of the loss will fall upon the women who are expected to be the chief gainers in so great a change. In virtue of their subject nature, they now hold the Godward side of humanity, which is, in fact, the side of highest power; and abjuring their nature they, of course, abjure the power.[58]

The above citation illustrates that Bushnell attempted to persuade women to return to their proper nature by appealing to his authority as a minister. By utilizing his authority as a clergyman, he also attempted to bring women into the church, and by doing so, he hoped to build a Christian America.

Summary of This Section

Bushnell supported women when it came to public preaching in the church. Preaching, however, did not automatically lead to women's administration in his mind, because he believed that women's administration threatened the patriarchal and hierarchical order of men and women in the church (i.e., men's government and women's subordination). Yet, Bushnell regarded the role of the deaconess as very important, and felt that the deaconess should be in "common ministry" with pastors. Based on the above, it seems that Bushnell wanted women to stay in the church and religiously participate in building a Christian America through their work as preachers and deaconesses. This was essential activity because, in his view, women were religiously superior to men.

The Minister's Wife

Susan Hill Lindley notes that the minister's wife was neglected by traditional church historians, yet was crucial to the lives of the church of nineteenth-century America.[59] In this section, I will attempt to clarify how Bushnell viewed the role of the minister's wife. I will also discuss how Mary Apthorp Bushnell, Bushnell's wife, fit into that role.

Sweet's Description of Four Models of the Minister's Wife

Leonard I. Sweet describes four models of the minister's wife that existed from the seventeenth century to the nineteenth century: the Companion model, the Sacrificer model, the Assistant model, and the Partner model.[60] Sweet divides the Companion model into that of the "yoke fellow" and the "helpmeet."[61] He says that ministers' wives as yoke fellows were obedient to their husbands and had no public involvement or visibility.[62] In the eighteenth century, the minister's wife as "helpmeet" replaced the image of "yoke fellow." Helpmeets were transitional figures that tentatively participated in the ministry through visitation, women's prayer meetings and other activities.[63] Sweet explains that the Sacrificer model included the wife who was removed from her husband's ministry and focused on raising their family on her own. On the other hand, the Assistant wife was a woman who shared many pastoral responsibilities and functioned as an extension of her husband's ministry. Finally, the Partner was a wife who not only performed ministerial tasks, but also developed various ministries with her husband.[64]

Some Ministers' Wives Invaded Their Husbands' Sphere

Lois A. Boyd portrays nineteenth-century American Presbyterian ministers' wives as being good wives and mothers, indefatigable church workers, appropriate and pious in behavior, and supporters of their husbands' concerns.[65] She also points out that in actuality ministers' wives transcended the rigid sphere assigned to women.[66] Julie Roy Jeffrey, in writing about Methodist clergy wives on the frontier, notes that "the boundary between female 'lay' and male 'clerical' efforts was, in practice, often hazy. Clearly also, some clergy wives encroached upon . . . male prerogatives."[67] Although Boyd focuses on Presbyterian ministers' wives, and Jeffrey concentrates on frontier Methodist clergy wives, the similarity between the two types of women was that these ministers' wives were beginning to encroach upon their husbands' sphere.

Bushnell's Views of the Minister's Wife and Mary Apthorp Bushnell's Real Functions

In Chapter 2, I pointed out aspects of the relationship between Bushnell and his wife. I also demonstrated how their relationship was different from that of other husbands and wives, because of specific aspects unique to the relationship of a minister and his wife. A reading of Bushnell's letters clearly indicates that he understood how important the role of minister's wife was to a pastor.

In July, 1864, one of Bushnell's ministerial friends, Samuel Dutton of New Haven, lost his wife.[68] Bushnell wrote in a letter of condolence:

> Your much-loved wife is with you no more. . . . I believe that there is no man who so much feels the loss of a good wife as a Christian minister. She is in all his secrets. She is his only counsellor in things of daily occurrence, and there is no other to whom he can go. She preaches to him when nobody else will, and preaches sometimes through him, when he would not, or what he would not, by himself. She chastises his faults with a dear and tender fidelity when nobody else can. In these and a hundred other ways she gets twisted and twined into everything that belongs to his life and life-work. So, I know, you will have found it. But it will be one very great comfort, and you will thank God for it, that her work is not ended, but still remains. You know now what she would say and do, and your life is just so much enlarged by her still.[69]

In 1869, Bushnell dedicated his book, *Women's Suffrage; The Reform Against Nature*, to his wife. In his acknowledgment, he praised his wife in the following manner:

> She has been with me in many weaknesses and some storms, giving strength alike in both; sharp enough to see my faults, faithful enough to expose them, and considerate enough to do it wisely; shrinking never from loss, or blame, or shame to be encountered in any thing right to be done; adding great and high instigations—instigations always to good, and never to evil mistaken for good; forecasting always things bravest and best to be done, and supplying inspirations enough to have made a hero, if they had not lacked the timber. . . . [These] compelling [compel] me thus to honor not less, but more, the covert glory of the womanly nature; even as I obtain a distincter, and more wondering apprehension of the divine meanings, and moistenings, and countless, unbought ministries, it contributes to this otherwise very dry world.[70]

Hence, Bushnell believed that a minister's wife was a counselor to her husband, a person who knew all his secrets, a special preacher to him, a faithful and tender-hearted chastiser of his faults, a companion, and someone who was courageous, instigative, predictive, and inspirational. In short, Bushnell's expectation of a minister's wife was, above all, a woman who realized her general nature, and more specifically, realized her religious nature.[71] In this sense, it seems that Bushnell's image of a minister's wife was not basically different from his general image of a woman. However, this does not mean that Bushnell did not recognize the importance of the clergy wife. For him, the minister's wife enabled her husband to carry out his ministry in a an effective manner.

As noted in Chapter 2, Bushnell expected his wife to be his "fellow soldier" for Christianity in the common errand God had given them. In other words, he expected her to join with him as they triumphantly moved forward with the ministry of Christianity.[72]

For instance, in 1846 Bushnell requested his wife's suggestion about his preaching:

> My text this morning was, "A Man's life consisteth not in the abundance of the things that he possesseth." . . . If you have anything to suggest that will help me, let me have it by mail or telegraph. . . . I wish I had you here to talk out the matter.[73]

In 1852, he thanked Mary Apthorp Bushnell for reporting on the prayer meeting in his church. He noted, "I cannot tell you what joy it gave me to hear the news you report concerning the church,—the day prayer-meeting, and the Thursday evening prayer-meeting."[74] In addition, he wrote to his wife in 1856, "I am very glad to hear you speak so encouragingly of our prayer-meeting."[75]

Robert L. Edwards notes that Bushnell's wife had the ability to perform ministerial duties as necessary. For instance, while Bushnell was in California in 1856, she filled in for him in various parish tasks, such as visitations, entertaining, and forming a new Bible class, "for which she already had at hand a lesson guide she had published on the life of Christ."[76] In addition, Bushnell's wife—along with Mary Beecher Perkins, John Olmsted's wife and others—served on a committee that hired a new principal and advised her on the development of the Hartford Female Seminary.[77]

Utilizing the models provided by Leonard I. Sweet, one can see that Bushnell's views of the minister's wife and the functions of Mary Apthorp Bushnell belong to the Companion Model, and more specifically to the model of "helpmeet." Therefore, Bushnell's expectations for his wife were not quite as old-fashioned as the "yoke fellow" views. In addition, Mary Apthorp Bushnell was not a retiring woman in her role as clergy wife, but in reality was rather active.[78] However, it is not accurate to say that Bushnell's wife was beginning to encroach on his sphere in the sense that Boyd suggests Presbyterian ministers' wives transcended the rigidity of "woman's sphere," and the way that Jeffrey contends some frontier-based Methodist ministers' wives invaded their husband's sphere.

In addition, a comparison of Bushnell and his wife with Charles G. Finney (1792-1875) and his wives, reveals that Bushnell's views of a minister's wife and Mary Apthorp Bushnell's role were not as up-to-date as those of Finney and his wives. Bushnell and Finney were friends, although they differed on many points as pastors and theologians. Charles Finney and his first wife, Lydia Finney, transformed the idea of a minister's wife from the "helpmeet" model to the Assistant model.[79] Furthermore, Finney and Elizabeth Atkinson Finney, his second wife, promoted the role of the minister's wife to that of Partner in ministry.[80] Thus, Finney and his wives were conscious of the significance of equality with regard to the ministry of the pastor and his wife.

However, even though his perspective differed from Finney's, Bushnell still viewed the clergyman's wife as important to the church, and hoped to bring her into the ministry of the church. Bushnell understood that her activities would help transform the American nation into a Christian America.

Women in Bushnell's Congregation

Women's Presence in the Nineteenth-Century American Church
Richard D. Shiels points out that women represented the majority of church membership in nineteenth-century America, specifically in New England Congregational churches. Shiels also notes that the percentage of New England women joining the church rose dramatically after 1800; and that by 1835, the percentage of women belonging to churches was double the percentage of the male population belonging to churches.[81] In addition, David G. Hackett states that from 1850 to 1890, the number of Protestants in America nearly tripled, and that during that same period, two-thirds of all Protestants were women.[82]

Women's Presence in Bushnell's Congregation
What then was the ratio of women and men in Bushnell's congregation? Robert L. Edwards notes, "From the founding of the parish to the time of Bushnell's departure, they [the women of the North Congregational Church of Hartford] were in a substantial majority, between sixty-three and sixty-seven percent."[83] Barbara Cross also suggests that the women in Bushnell's congregation constituted a large percentage of the church membership.[84] Based on the evidence above, it is clear that the percentage of women in Bushnell's congregation reflected the national percentage of female churchgoers in nineteenth-century America.

Women in Bushnell's Congregation
There were various kinds of women in Bushnell's congregation. Among them were Mrs. William Ely, widow of a successful Dutch East Indies merchant, and Mary Beecher Perkins, the wife of lawyer, Thomas C. Perkins.[85] Mary Beecher Perkins was a graduate of Miss Pierce's School in Litchfield, Connecticut[86] and taught at the Hartford Female Seminary. In 1827 she married Thomas C. Perkins, and continued her life as a devoted wife and mother. Despite Mary Beecher Perkins' earlier career as a teacher, the Perkins family was uninvolved in controversial issues such as abolition and women's rights.[87] Margaret K. Jordan was also a member of Bushnell's congregation. Her husband, Octavius, designed a mansion for Samuel Colt, the famous arms manufacturer. Mary L. Steele, on the other hand, ran a

boarding house. Elizabeth D. Apthop, Bushnell's unmarried sister-in-law (who was not a church member, but a regular attendee during the 1850s), managed an exclusive school for girls.[88]

Mary Lyman Collins, the wife of Amos M. Collins (who was a merchant, Hartford mayor for two terms, and a senior deacon for most of Bushnell's ministry), was a member of the North Congregational Church. Both husband and wife supported Bushnell, especially during the difficult time when he was criticized by other Hartford ministers. Mary Lyman Collins worked for the Widows Society, planned for the "Mothers' Meeting" (the Maternal Association), and taught a Bible class. She also participated in mission work in Hartford and made visits of charity to the inmates of the Hartford jail, in addition to involving herself in many church activities. She also filled the office of "Monthly Visitor" at the Retreat for the Insane. During the Civil War, she ministered to the needs of the soldiers.[89]

Bushnell wrote a description of Amos M. and Mary Lyman Collins in 1873, at the request of their grandson, Rev. Charles Terry Collins. Bushnell's comments on Mary Lyman Collins make it clear that he viewed women's charitable work as important for both the church and society. He wrote:

> Her [Mary Lyman Collins'] Society for Widows and the little Societies of Want in the poor families did not forget what it was in her heart to do for them, coming surely for help to her, as to a bureau of Providence always accessible. It was not so much her bent to be a missionary, as to be a broadly Christian woman. It seemed, in fact, to be agreed between her husband and herself that they should keep house for God; and they turned away never the fugitive from their door; they laid in stores for charity; they maintained, with admirable patience, an almost open state of hospitality, at which a large ministerial acquaintance, and reformers in transit and strangers arrived on errands of beneficence were their guests.[90]

Based on the above, it is obvious that Bushnell regarded women's charity as a means of God's grace. This is further confirmed by comments made in one of his important letters to his daughters. In the missive, he tried to open their eyes to the plight of poor people and advised the girls to be merciful.[91] Additionally, Bushnell conceived the role of deaconess as an important part of women's ministry.

However, based on the rule of the church, the women of Bushnell's congregation could not vote and were excluded from administration. One of their functions was to make "annual house-to-house rounds to raise funds for mission enterprises."[92] In terms of their administrative responsibilities, they were quite limited. They were entrusted to raise money, but could not decide how that money would be spent.

In short, the women in Bushnell's congregation reflected what he taught about women's roles in the church--that is, they undertook charitable works, because Bushnell hoped and believed that the American nation would grow strong through women's participation in religious activity. However, the women in his congregation also reflected his view of women in general. In other words, they could not vote in the church and were excluded from the administrative decision-making.

Summary of This Chapter

In this chapter, I have argued that Bushnell entrusted a strong church foundation to women, rather than to men. By making use of women—especially their religious nature, preaching, deaconess work, and clergy wife participation in ministry—Bushnell hoped to form a solid church that would lead to the Christianization of the nation. His desire was to transform America into a Christian America in a religious, rather than a political way, and he believed that this could be accomplished through women's religious activities in the church. At the same time, Bushnell rejected women's administration, because it would threaten the patriarchal and hierarchical order of men and women. Thus, it is clear that his views of women in the church were rather complex.

The Next Chapter

In the next chapter, "Women in the Nation," I argue that Bushnell was afraid that women's participation in politics via the right to vote would weaken the foundations of family, church, and nation, and would lead to the decline of a Christian America based on the organic unity of family, church, and nation. And yet, except for the case of women's participation in the political field, Bushnell believed that women's sphere ought to be expanded much more in society. In this sense, his views on the relationships between women and men were egalitarian. Thus, Bushnell's views also showed complexity regarding the sphere of women in society.

Notes

1 Horace Bushnell, *Women's Suffrage; The Reform Against Nature* (New York: Charles Scribner and Company, 1869), 59.

2 Ibid., 57.

3 In *Christian Nurture*, Bushnell noted the relationship between Law and Gospel: "Law and gospel have a natural relationship and they are bound together every where, by a firm interior necessity. . . . The law of God is finally melted into the heart by the cross of Jesus." See Horace Bushnell, *Christian Nurture* (New York: Charles Scribner, 1861; reprint, Grand Rapids: Baker Book House, 1979), 357-58.

4 Bushnell, *Women's Suffrage; The Reform Against Nature*, 65.

5 Ibid., 65-66.

6 Ibid., 66.

7 Ibid., 66-67.

8 Mary Bushnell Cheney, ed., *Life and Letters of Horace Bushnell* (New York: Harper & Brothers, Publishers, 1880; reprint, New York: Arno Press & *The New York Times*, 1969), 193.

9 Ibid., 358.

10 Bushnell, *Christian Nurture*, 360.

11 John Kent points out, "Daphne Hampson, a feminist theologian, argues that the central Christian theme of sacrifice, salvation through suffering, might appeal to the male warrior but not to the woman who has freed herself from male role-models." That is, concepts such as sacrifice and suffering which Bushnell regarded as crucial, do not attract contemporary feminists. See John Kent, "The Character and Possibility of Christian Theology Today," in *Companion Encyclopedia of Theology*, 1995.

12 Horace Bushnell, *Nature and the Supernatural, as together Constituting the One System of God* (New York: Charles Scribner, 1858), 296-97. See also Horace Bushnell, *The Character of Jesus: Forbidding his Possible Classification with Men* (New York: Charles Scribner, 1861), 46-47.

13 Horace Bushnell, *The Vicarious Sacrifice, Grounded in Principles of Universal Obligation* (New York: Charles Scribner & Co., 1866), 42.

14 Ibid., 46.

15 Ibid., 47.

16 Horace Bushnell, *Forgiveness and Law, Grounded in Principles* (New York: Scribner, Armstrong & Co., 1874), 19.

17 Cheney, ed., 541-42. Bushnell also considered that there should be two modes of love, that is, Christian love and artistic love. According to him, artistic love does not require self-sacrifice, but Christian love should include self-sacrifice. Ibid., 435-36.

In addition, Bushnell's understanding of love was rather complex. Sometimes he understood that love did not necessarily need to include vicarious sacrifice itself, while sometimes he understood that love should always include vicarious sacrifice. It is also true that Bushnell was interested in seeing and loving Christ artistically. That is why he is sometimes understood as a Transcendentalist. However, it is not correct to conclude that Bushnell was a Transcendentalist. The concept of vicarious sacrifice in love best expresses Bushnell's characteristic as a theologian.

18 Cheney, ed., 544.

19 Elizabeth Cady Stanton et al., *The Woman's Bible: Part II, Comments on the Old and New Testaments from Joshua to Revelation* (New York: European Publishing Company, 1898), 131.

20 Interestingly enough, Bushnell did not mention Eve at all in his works regarding either women's general nature or women's religious nature.

21 Bushnell, *Women's Suffrage; The Reform Against Nature*, 58, 61.

22 Cheney, ed., 505.

23 Cheney, ed., 505.

24 Horace Bushnell, "Mary, the Mother of Jesus," in *Sermons on Living Subjects* (New York: Charles Scribner's Sons, 1872), 10.

25 Ibid., 10.

26 Ibid., 16.

27 Ibid., 36.

28 Ibid., 31.

29 Ibid., 34.

30 Ibid., 35.

31 Horace Bushnell, "The Insight of Love," in *Christ and His Salvation: In Sermons Variously Related Thereto* (New York: Charles Scribner, 1864), 51.

32 Ibid., 61.

33 Ibid., 60.

34 Ibid., 68-69.

35 Susan Hill Lindley, *"You Have Stept Out Of Your Place": A History of Women and Religion in America* (Louisville: Westminster John Knox Press, 1996), 117.

36 Lindley, 122.

37 Ibid., 122. Donald W. Dayton treats Phoebe Palmer as a significant, although neglected, figure who defended the right of women to preach in his "The Evangelical Roots of Feminism" chapter. See Donald W. Dayton, *Discovering An Evangelical Heritage* (Peabody: Hendrickson Publishers, Inc., 1976), 96. Regarding Phoebe Palmer as feminist, see Charles Edward White, *The Beauty of Holiness: Phoebe Palmer as Theologian, Revivalist, Feminist, and Humanitarian* (Grand Rapids: Francis Asbury Press, 1986), 205-06. White notes that Palmer was mildly supportive of the women who wanted political and legal rights; but she did not discuss all the facets of the women's rights movement of her era. Instead, she focused only on "the right of women to exercise all their gifts in the church." If women followed her advice, then Palmer believed that the world would be greatly changed. See White, 206.

38 Lindley, 123-24. See also Elizabeth Cazden, *Antoinette Brown Blackwell: A Biography* (New York: The Feminist Press, 1983), 86.

39 Ibid., 128.

40 Ibid., 128.

41 Ibid., 131-32.

---

42 Barbara Brown Zikmund, "The Struggle for the Right to Preach," in *Women and Religion in America: The Nineteenth Century*, ed. Rosemary Radford Ruether and Rosemary Skinner Keller (San Francisco: Harper & Row, Publishers, 1981), 193-205.

43 Ibid., 205.

44 Jeannine E. Olson, *One Ministry[,] Many Roles: Deacons and Deaconesses through the Centuries* (St. Louis: Concordia Publishing House, 1992), 19.

45 Ibid., 253, 271.

46 Ibid., 286.

47 Bushnell, *Women's Suffrage; The Reform Against Nature*, 181-82.

48 Ibid., 21-22.

49 Bushnell, *Women's Suffrage; The Reform Against Nature*, 22.

50 Ibid., 24.

51 Ibid., 24. See also 25. In 1845, Bushnell wrote a very important letter to his daughter from Europe. In that letter he said, "You cannot be a soldier or a preacher." However, he should have said, "You cannot be a soldier or a pastor," because he actually accepted women's public preaching in church. See Cheney, ed., 140.

52 Bushnell, *Women's Suffrage; The Reform Against Nature*, 24.

53 Ibid., 21.

54 Ibid., 24.

55 Bushnell, *Women's Suffrage; The Reform Against Nature*, 23-24.

56 Ibid., 25. See also 22. According to Beverly Gaventa, a biblical scholar, Phoebe is actually misnamed as a "deaconess," for the Greek is more accurately rendered as "deacon," indicating that Phoebe had an important role in the church that did not significantly differ from the roles of the male leaders. See Beverly Roberts Gaventa, "Romans," in *The Women's Bible Commentary*, ed. Carol A. Newsom and Sharon H. Ringe (Louisville: Westminster/John Knox Press, 1992), 320.

57 Bushnell, *Women's Suffrage; The Reform Against Nature*, 182.

58 Ibid., 182.

59 Lindley, 68.

60 Leonard I. Sweet, *The Minister's Wife: Her Role in Nineteenth-Century American Evangelicalism* (Philadelphia: Temple University Press, 1983), 3.

61 Ibid., 5.

62 Ibid., 5.

63 Ibid., 5.

64 Ibid., 3.

65 Lois A. Boyd, "Presbyterian Ministers' Wives: A Nineteenth-Century Portrait," *Journal of Presbyterian History* 59 (1981): 15.

66 Ibid., 3-4.

67 Julie Roy Jeffrey, "Ministry Through Marriage: Methodist Clergy Wives on the Trans-Mississippi Frontier," in *Women in New Worlds: Historical Perspectives on the Wesleyan Tradition* vol. 1, ed. Hilah F. Thomas and Rosemary Skinner Keller (Nashville: Abingdon Press, 1981), 153.

68 Cheney, ed., 133.

69 Ibid., 483.

70 Bushnell, *Women's Suffrage; The Reform Against Nature*, no pagination.

71 About the religious nature of women, see "Religious Natures of Women and Men" in this chapter.

72 Cheney, ed., 275. See also Chapter 2.

73 Ibid., 176.

74 Cheney, ed., 274. T. H. Olbricht explains, "Prayer meetings are mentioned occasionally before 1800, but were popularized by Charles G. Finney and Dwight L. Moody. . . . Among seventeenth-century Puritans, regular

gatherings were Sunday morning and evening, and Thursday morning for a lecture." See T. H. Olbricht, "Prayer Meeting," in *Dictionary of Christianity in America*, 1990.

75 Cheney, ed., 375.

76 Edwards, *Of Singular Genius, Of Singular Grace*, 264. However, Edwards is inconsistent because in another work he stated that Mary was quietly with Bushnell. Edwards notes, "It is hard to imagine Horace Bushnell being all the preacher and leader he was without his Mary being quietly there with him." See Edwards, *The Prow of the Ship: Preachers and Preaching over 150 Years* (Hartford: The Bond Press Incorporated, 1979), 9. Stanley B. Weld says, "She [Mary, Bushnell's wife] proved a great help to him [Bushnell]." See Stanley B. Weld, *The History of Immanuel Church, 1824-1967* (Hartford: Connecticut Printers, Incorporated, 1968), 14.

77 Edwards, *Of Singular Genius, Of Singular Grace*, 264.

78 Randolph Crump Miller considers Bushnell's wife to be "a supporting companion throughout his [Bushnell's] career." See Randolph Crump Miller, "Horace Bushnell: Prophet to America's Children," *Perkins Journal* 32 (1979): 1. Robert L. Edwards sees Bushnell's wife as "an active, working partner." See Edwards, *Of Singular Genius, Of Singular Grace*, 264. Stanley B. Weld regards Bushnell's wife as "a fellow worker." See Weld, *The History of Immanuel Church, 1824-1967*, 14.

79 Sweet, 76.

80 Ibid., 10, 184-211. See also Charles E. Hambrick-Stowe, *Charles G. Finney and the Spirit of American Evangelicalism* (Grand Rapids: William B. Eerdmans Publishing Company, 1996), 235.

81 Richard D. Shiels, "The Feminization of American Congregationalism, 1730-1835," *American Quarterly* 39 (1981): 51-52. See also J. William T. Youngs, *The Congregationalists* (New York: Greenwood Press, 1990), 128.

82 David G. Hackett, "Gender and Religion in American Culture, 1870-1930," *Religion and American Culture* 5, no. 2 (Summer 1995): 132.

83 Robert L. Edwards, "Portrait of a People: Horace Bushnell's Hartford Congregation," in *Studies of the Church in History*, ed. Horton Davies (Allison Park: Pickwick Publications, 1983), 154.

84 Barbara M. Cross, *Horace Bushnell: Minister to a Changing America* (Chicago: The University of Chicago Press, 1958), Chapter 4. See also Ronald William Hogeland, "Femininity and the Nineteenth Century Post-Puritan Mind" (Ph.D. diss., University of California, Los Angeles, 1968), 250.

85 Edwards, *Of Singular Genius, Of Singular Grace*, 139.

86 Milton Rugoff notes, "Although it had a full academic curriculum, a primary aim of Miss Pierce's academy, not unlike that of later 'finishing schools,' was to teach decorum, ladylike manners and 'refined conversation'—in short, the social graces." See Milton Rugoff, *The Beechers: An American Family in the Nineteenth Century* (New York: Harper & Row, Publishers, 1981), 43.

87 Joseph S. Van Why, "Crusaders of the Pen and Podium: Henry Ward Beecher, Thomas K. Beecher and Other Family Members," in *Portraits of a Nineteenth Century Family: A Symposium on the Beecher Family*, ed. Earl A. French and Diana Royce (Hartford: The Stowe-Day Foundation, 1976), 111.

88 Edwards, "Portrait of a People: Horace Bushnell's Hartford Congregation," 154.

89 Clarence Lyman Collens, *Collins Memorial* (NP: Clarence Lyman Collens, 1959), 24.

90 Ibid., 29.

91 Cheney, ed., 273. See also Chapter 2.

92 Edwards, "Portrait of a People: Horace Bushnell's Hartford Congregation," 154.

CHAPTER 4
WOMEN IN THE NATION

Christian America

Bushnell's Definition of a Christian America

Bushnell desired a Christian America. However, his idea of a Christian America requires definition. He said, "I say not or believe, that Christendom will be Puritanized, or Protestantized; but what is better than either, it will be Christianized."[1] Ideally, Bushnell wanted to return to Puritan Christianity,[2] but realistically, he knew that the people of nineteenth-century America would not go back to a Puritan form of Christianity. Therefore, he suggested that people embrace a Christianized (or Christian) America—in short, a nation that endorsed basic Christian beliefs. He also suggested that a general Christian religion could lead America. Therefore, most of the time, he simply used the term "Christianity," rather than "Puritan Christianity" and/or "Protestant Christianity."

Organic Unity of the Family, Church, and Nation

In order to achieve the goal of Christian America, Bushnell understood that an organic unity needed to exist among the family, church, and nation.[3] Although he did not give a clear definition of "organic unity," it seems likely that his usage of the term indicated the unity that is found in a close, naturally occurring relationship. Bushnell felt that it was impossible for America to be a Christian nation without an organic unity of the three-fold structure.

This leads to the question of how family, church, and nation were organically united in Bushnell's thinking. First of all, with regard to the connectedness between family and church, he considered the family to be "a little church."[4] At the same time, he regarded the church as an enlarged family. In addition, Bushnell pointed to the close relationship between family and church by citing I Timothy 3:4: "For if a man know not how to rule his own house, how shall he take care of the church of God?"[5]

Regarding the connection between church and nation, Bushnell noted in 1835, "The whole frame-work of these free states, in short, and of this free nation, is drawn out from the bosom of the Church; or rather, it is the frame-work of the Church itself."[6] In 1861, he asked, "What has the church to do with the state? As if the state were really outside of God's prerogative and he had nothing to do with it!—nothing to do with the marshalling and well-ordering and protecting rule of society!"[7] Therefore, Bushnell understood that the nation was born out of the church and modeled after the church's structure. He also believed that God was intimately involved with social and governmental organizations.

Concerning the relationship between nation and family, it is clear Bushnell believed that the propagation of the family was necessary for building a strong American nation. However, it also should be noted that he seldom directly stated the relationship between nation and family. Instead, Bushnell inferred the close connection through the notion of "religious influence." For instance, in 1837, he remarked that a state should be grounded in religion, though the religion should not be established as a part of the political system.[8] He also stated in 1840, "I hope you [Bushnell's hearers] are at least impressed with a sense of the very intimate relation between politics and morals [religion] in our country."[9]

With regard to family and religion, Bushnell noted, "Home and religion are kindred words . . . home, because it is the seat of religion; religion, because it is the sacred element of home."[10] In addition, he said, "Religion never thoroughly penetrates life, till it becomes domestic. Like that patriotic fire which makes a nation invincible, it never burns with inextinguishable devotion till it burns at the hearth."[11] In short, he believed that nation and family were closely aligned by the function of religious influence. Thus, one of the important characteristics of Bushnell's thought is that family, church, and nation are organically united with one another.

Bushnell's Organicism and the Spread of Individualism

Bushnell's idea of the organic unity of family, church, and nation led to his emphasis on the importance of the concept of organicism. Daniel Walker Howe points out that Bushnell's conservative organicism became apparent as early as the 1830s. He also explains that historians have traced the existence of "organicism" to the Civil War or to the 1850s. Based on Howe's observation, it seems that Bushnell formed his organicism much earlier than his contemporaries. Furthermore, Bushnell continued to endorse this notion for the rest of his life.[12]

Bushnell was led to organicism by the obvious spread of individualism in the American family, church, and nation during his lifetime.[13] He complained:

> All our modern notions and speculations have taken a bent toward individualism. . . . We have well nigh lost, as was to be expected, the idea of organic powers and relations. The state, the church, the family . . . become mere collections of units. . . . We only seem to lie as seeds piled together, without any terms of connection. . . . And thus the three great forms of organic existence, which God has appointed for the race, are in fact lost out of mental recognition.[14]

Thus, Bushnell was frustrated by the prevalence of individualism, and stressed the importance of organicism by urging people to embrace the significance of the organic unity of family, church, and nation.

Mary Bushnell Cheney gives a succinct summary of her father's argument in support of organicism and against individualism:

> It [*Christian Nurture*] is opposed to the *Individualism* of the then prevalent theology [Revivalism], and recognizes and emphasizes the *organic* life of the family, the Church and society at large, wherein no soul lives or acts alone as a unit, but all parts of a living organism, interdependent and mutually helpful.[15]

David L. Smith comments that Bushnell was sensitive to forces capable of destroying the unities of American society and thus disrupting the organic channels of community life through which Christianization could be possible.[16] Smith concludes, "In an age when individualism was common sense, Bushnell stood for the virtues of tradition and organic community."[17]

Two Ways for a Christian America

Bushnell wanted America to be built upon Christianity. He could not conceive that America could be a strong and growing nation without acknowledging Christianity. He thought that there were two ways in which a Christian America could be realized: one was by conversion, and the other was by way of family propagation.[18] Bushnell clearly preferred the latter, endorsing a Christian America that grew, not by the process of conversion, but "by the populating forces of a family grace in the church."[19] In short, he envisioned that a Christian America would come into existence not by the individualism of personal conversion, but by the organicism of the propagable unity of family, church, and nation.

Loyalty as a Link between the American Nation and Religion

In addition, Bushnell emphasized loyalty as an important attitude in his vision of a Christian America. According to Bushnell, loyalty was "his [man's] great sentiment, his deep and high devotion, the fire of his habitual or inborn homage to his country's welfare."[20] Loyalty functioned as a link between the idea of the American nation and the Christian religion. He stated:

> We believe . . . that the loyal man will be inclined towards religion by his public devotion, and the religious man raised in the temper of his loyalty to his country, by his religious devotion. The two fires will burn together and one will kindle the other.[21]

Thus, Bushnell saw a logical connection. The loyal patriot would turn to religion because he understood that religion provided the nation with a moral structure, and the religious man's devotion to his faith would lead him into the desire to do good and thereby he would participate in public acts of national loyalty.

A Future Christian America

Bushnell described a future Christian America in the following manner:

> We will not cease, till a christian [*sic*] nation throws up its temples of worship on every hill and plain; till knowledge, virtue and religion, blending their dignity and their healthful power, have filled our great country with a manly and a happy race of people, and the bands of a complete christian [*sic*] commonwealth are seen to span the continent.[22]

He firmly believed it would be possible for every single town to be populated with Christian people. In addition, he was convinced that the American nation would be made up of a "manly" people. That is, he could not imagine an effeminate American nation.

As for government, Bushnell placed hope for the current and future Christian America in the form of "a new republic." He wrote, "It is already clear to us that it was necessary for a new movement to begin. . . . A new republic must be planted, and must have time to grow."[23] Ideally speaking, he loved a monarchy as well as the New England fathers.[24] However, he realized that a monarchy would no longer be accepted in nineteenth-century America. He also did not want to give up the American government as a church-state system, because he understood that the American government ran its affairs according to the same principles and ways as the church.[25]

Politics, though, was not Bushnell's strong point. He was not a very devoted member of any political party.[26] Over the course of his life, he was first a Democrat, then later attracted to the Nationalist-Union party, and finally became a Republican.[27]

Bushnell and Women in Politics

All of the preceding leads to the question, "Where were women in Bushnell's vision of a Christian America?" The answer is: they were totally invisible in the political arena. He thoroughly rejected women's participation in politics by opposing women's suffrage. This opinion is crucial to Bushnell's process of building a Christian America. As mentioned previously, he envisioned that the American nation would be made up of "manly" people. In other words, he could not imagine a feminine American nation. Women, therefore, were either influencing events from the background or completely invisible.

New England Fathers and Revolutionary Fathers

The Birth of the American Nation

Bushnell thought that the birth of the American nation should be attributed to the New England fathers, rather than the Revolutionary fathers.[28] Robert L. Edwards notes, "For him [Bushnell], providential American history did not commence in 1776; it started with the Pilgrims and Puritans and evolved under God from that point."[29] Ultimately speaking, Bushnell considered God to be the Founder of the American nation. He wrote that God "is Founder before the founders, training both them and us, and building in the Constitution, before it is produced without. Our whole civil order is the ordinance of God."[30] In short, in Bushnell's mind, the nation needed to be a God-ordained institution. Furthermore, he believed that the American nation had commenced, not with the Revolutionary fathers, but the New England fathers.[31]

In *The Fathers of New England*,[32] Bushnell commented that "our fathers had as little thought of a separation from the mother country and as little desire of founding an independent commonwealth, as of the other distinctions. England was their home, they loved the monarchy."[33] Bushnell also believed that the reason the founders of New England left their homeland was religious, not political.[34] In other words, Bushnell understood that the New England fathers' true purpose in the New World was to complete the Reformation—not Luther's or Calvin's Reformation, but God's.[35]

In addition, Bushnell noted in *Reverses Needed*, "The political ideas of the New England fathers were shaped by religion—-so far church ideas. Government and the church were God's institutes—-ordinance of God."[36] He further noted, "They [The New England fathers] had no sehemes [schemes] of democracy to execute. They were not, in fact, or in their own view, republicans in their ideas of government."[37] In other words, Bushnell observed that the New England fathers never intended to create a republican form of government. Bushnell, moreover, saw that the New England fathers did not consider instituting the separation of church and state: "They as little thought of raising a separation of church and state as of planting a new democracy."[38]

A Crisis in American History: The Revolutionary Fathers

In Bushnell's opinion, the American nation passed through three crises.[39] One of them was the era of the Revolutionary fathers.[40] Bushnell noted:

> It [the element of the Revolutionary fathers] was represented by Thomas Jefferson: a man who taught abstractively, not religiously. . . . He had no conception of difficulty in making a complete government by mere human composition; following Rousseau's theory, which discovers the foundation of all government in a "social compact."[41]

Thus, Bushnell was critical to Jefferson. Bushnell wrote that theoretically, "We had New England and Virginia, Puritan church order and the doctrine of the French Encyclopedia, fused happily together in the language of Thomas Jefferson."[42] However, Bushnell saw that in reality, problems arose when the two elements—ideas of the New England fathers and the ideas of the Revolutionary fathers—entered into the political order during the Revolution. The two types of thought caused confusion between a social compact and God's ordinance in terms of the foundation of government.[43] This is why Bushnell saw the Revolutionary era as a crisis in the history of the American nation.[44]

Another Crisis in American History: Women's Suffrage Movement

It is evident that Bushnell also understood the women's suffrage movement to be another serious crisis in American history. Theoretically, the women's suffrage movement was related to the social compact theory of government and the belief that all human beings had natural rights, the same concepts that were important to the Revolutionary fathers (especially Thomas Jefferson). It is precisely because women's suffrage located itself within the social compact theory of government and argued for suffrage on the basis of inalienable, natural human rights that Bushnell opposed the movement.

The suffragists, on the other hand, did not perceive the Revolutionary fathers as leaders who caused a crisis in American history. Rather, leaders such as Elizabeth Cady Stanton, Susan B. Anthony, and Mary Ann McClintock acknowledged their ideological continuity with the leadership of the American Revolution.[45]

Women's Suffrage

Women in Nineteenth-Century America, and the Seneca Falls Convention

The condition of women in nineteenth-century American society was restrictive with regard to rights. Harry L. Watson provides the following succinct description of females in nineteenth-century America:

> Jacksonian equality did not apply to women. In every state, women were denied the right to vote and hold office. Married women could not own property or sign contracts because the law submerged their identities in the persons of their husbands. Divorce was almost impossible, especially for wives. Women were routinely barred from higher education and most responsible professions.[46]

As a response to these conditions, a group of women held what came to be known as the Seneca Falls Convention on July 19-20, 1848. Out of that gathering came the Declaration of Seneca Falls, issued by Lucretia Mott, Martha C. Wright, Elizabeth Cady Stanton, and Mary Ann McClintock.[47] The Declaration of Seneca Falls self-consciously modeled its construction and language after the Declaration of Independence:

> We hold these truths to be self-evident: that all men and women are created equal; that they are endowed by their Creator with certain inalienable rights. . . . He[Man] has never permitted her[woman] to exercise her inalienable right to the elective franchise. . . . Having deprived her of this first right of a citizen, the elective franchise, thereby, leaving her without representation in the halls of legislation, he has oppressed her on all sides. . . . In the covenant of marriage, she is compelled to promise obedience to her husband, he becoming, to all intents and purposes, her master. . . . He has monopolized nearly all the profitable employments. . . . He has denied her the facilities for obtaining a thorough education, all colleges being closed against her. He allows her in Church, as well as State, but a subordinate position, claiming Apostolic authority for her exclusion from the ministry, and, with some exception, from any public participation in the affairs of the Church.[48]

Women's Anti-Suffrage Movement

It is interesting to note that nationally organized opposition to women's suffrage did not immediately follow the 1848 Convention.[49] Furthermore, when the organized backlash came, it did not come from men. According to Susan E. Marshall, in 1871, a group of nineteen women published a petition to the U.S. Congress that argued against female suffrage.[50] Marshall also notes that the petitioners "justified their position on the basis of Holy Scripture, female physical frailty, children's welfare, marital stability, and social order."[51] Furthermore, she observes that Bushnell was one of the persons who provided the foundation for the argument against women's suffrage,[52] although Marshall does not explain how Bushnell did this.

Women's Suffrage and Women's Anti-Suffrage in Connecticut

In Connecticut, where Bushnell lived as a pastor and theologian and spoke out against women's suffrage, a minority of the Committee on Constitutional Amendments to the legislature of Connecticut agreed with the issue of women's suffrage and reported on women's enfranchisement in 1868.[53] In September, 1869, Isabella Beecher Hooker, along with John Hooker (Isabella's attorney husband), Francis Ellen Burr, and other leading citizens, issued the call for Connecticut's first women's suffrage convention. The convention was held that same year.[54] Among the participants were Paulina Wright Davis, Julia Ward Howe, Susan B. Anthony, Elizabeth Cady Stanton, Henry Ward Beecher, Harriet Beecher Stowe, Catharine Beecher, William Lloyd Garrison, and the Reverend Olympia Brown.[55] Of these people, Bushnell knew Henry Ward Beecher, Harriet Beecher Stowe, and Catharine Beecher very well.

Catharine Beecher and Harriet Beecher Stowe, however, later withdrew their support for women's suffrage, because they were "conservative" in their views on the woman question.[56] Unlike their brother, Henry Ward Beecher, the two sisters were reluctant to give women the right to vote. According to Catharine Beecher, women's roles were the conservation of the home, guarding and developing the human body in infancy, and education of the children.[57] She later became one of the signers of the first anti-suffrage petition in 1871.[58] From Harriet Beecher Stowe's perspective, men needed to be the moral, physical and intellectual head of women. She also was convinced that women's duty was to inculcate their children with the Christian values of self-sacrifice and self-denial.[59]

John Hooker prepared the resolutions for the 1869 pro-suffrage convention. According to Nichols, the resolutions "called for a broad range of reforms, from political and property rights to increased educational and employment opportunities for women." Nichols additionally notes that the group also declared that male/female equality was God's intention for the creation of a perfect society.[60]

As a result of the convention, the Connecticut Woman Suffrage Association (CWSA) was formed in 1869.[61] In the principal address at the October 1869 meeting, Henry Ward Beecher pressed for female suffrage and the right to hold office.[62] Bushnell understood Beecher to be a man whose support for women's suffrage was rooted in the belief that it would refine society.[63]

On the other hand, opponents of women's suffrage in Connecticut declared that the right to vote was not a natural right, and that the Government did not derive its power from the consent of the governed. They also stressed that enfranchising women would not elevate the character of office-holders, would not purify politics, would not render the laws more equitable, would not give a protection to women, would not open up more occupations, and would not insure a reconstruction of the statute laws.[64]

Bushnell as a Consistent Anti-Suffragist

Bushnell was a consistent anti-suffragist throughout his life. This is evident in many of his remarks. Not only are anti-suffrage comments found in *Women's Suffrage; The Reform Against Nature* written in 1869 (one of his last works), but they are also found in one of his earliest works, "American Politics," written in 1840.[65] It is interesting to note that Bushnell penned "American Politics" eight years before the Seneca Falls Convention. In this essay, he observed:

> If that revolution [women's suffrage] goes on as it has begun, it will certainly destroy some of the most precious and best influences we have left. Do save us one half of society free of the broils, and bruises, and arts of demagogy! Let us have a place of quiet, and some quiet minds which the din of our public war never embroils. Let a little of the sweetness, purity, and of the simple religion of life remain. God made the woman to be a help for man, not to be wrestler with him. This he declared in the grand sacrament of creation, and we have a greater interest in the arrangement, as religious beings.[66]

Thus, Bushnell regarded women's suffrage as a revolution in American history, but understood it as a revolution in the negative sense. He also believed that the political world in which men were engaged was noisy and dirty. He entreated women not to wrestle politically with men. Indeed, he urged them not to venture into the noisy, dirty political world at all. Rather, he asked women to remain in a quiet, pure religious life, and to help their husbands. In fact, he firmly believed that God did not create women to be co-wrestlers in the world with men, but to be men's help-meets. From Bushnell's point of view, it was women's nature that they were created, not as political leaders, but as men's assistants.

Bushnell's Arguments against Women's Suffrage

Bushnell considered the following arguments as subtle, but prevalent mistakes about women's suffrage and he refuted them. He rejected the argument that "woman should not be in any sense more complementary to man than man to woman."[67] He believed that a woman was created to be the "meet-helper" of the man—that is, to be subsidiary to the man.[68] In support of his position, Bushnell cited the Apostle Paul in the New Testament: "Neither was the man created for the woman, but the woman for the man."[69]

Bushnell strongly opposed the notion that "as culture reduced the distinctness of the sexes, we were to presume a final obliteration of their distinguishing qualities, and turn both sexes into the great field of public action together."[70] He insisted that neither manly women, nor womanly men ought to be encouraged.[71] He was afraid that, if women's suffrage came to be, then "manly women" and "womanly men" would appear in large numbers. In other words, he worried that the distinctions between the sexes would be blurred by women's suffrage. He concluded, "The man will be manlier, that he has a true womanly wife, and the wife will be the more womanly, that she has a manly husband. Develop both natures to the utmost, and the development of each will help that of the other."[72] Thus, Bushnell clearly was uneasy with the notion of blurring gender distinctions. He fully expected men/husbands to be manly, and women/wives to be womanly, not vice versa.

Bushnell also rejected the prevalent argument that women should have the right to vote in order to refine society. He noted that Henry Ward Beecher, his contemporary, supported this belief:

> Since the world began, to refine society has been woman's function. She is God's vicegerent on earth, for that end. You may be sure that she that has carried refinement to the household, to the church, to social life, to literature, to art, to every interest except government, will also carry it to legislation, and the whole of civil and public procedure, if it is to be carried there at all.[73]

However, Bushnell argued the converse: if women went into political life, then they would spoil the delicacy of their subject nature, become unrefined, and be more like men.[74]

He also thought that Harriet Taylor Mill, a wife of John Stuart Mill, understood women to be "passing through life in a state of forced subordination to the other half."[75] However, Bushnell saw this view as an inversion of the true argument. For him, the subordination of women had never been forced. He declared, "The subordination is moral simply based, that is, in moral expression."[76]

Bushnell also noted that the American people confused the idea of authority with that of "dictation-force (command enforced by sanction)."[77] In addition, when he used the term "authority," he used it two ways: men's political authority and women's authority. He believed that women's authority should have a softer element developed in a more sheltered way of life, making it different and much more complete than male authority.[78] He further argued that if a woman went after male or political authority, "hoping to win it by the sublime rage of a candidacy, she would come out *minus*, even in her victory, to be no authority at all."[79]

Thus, Bushnell perceived that the valid place for women's authority was the home. On the other hand, he did not reject the notion of women participating in the activities outside the home, as described later in this chapter. Therefore, he possessed complex views regarding the place of women's authority.

Suffrage consists of voting and holding offices. Bushnell began his argument by discussing the right of women to vote. He rejected the claim that women and men were equal and that, therefore, women had an equal right to vote.[80] Instead, he argued that women had a perfect right to be women, just as men had a perfect right to be men; but having a perfect right to be either women or men did not extend to the right to vote.[81]

Bushnell viewed men and women as "unlike in kind."[82] He stated:

> It is not certainly true that women are equal to men. They are equally women as men are men; they are equally human as men . . . [B]ut it does not hence appear that they are equal to men. They may be superior to men; they may be inferior to men; but what is a great deal closer probably to the truth, they may be very unlike in kind to men. . . . Accordingly, if the two sexes are so very unlike in *kind*, there can, so far, be no predication of equality between them.[83]

To make his point, he observed that a yard and a pound were both forms of measurement, but "have no common quality." Likewise, he pointed out that silk and flax were fabric threads, but very different. He then drew a parallel between men and women, arguing, "While women and men have a great many common properties, they have also a great many which are not common—so many, that we never can be sure what we mean by it, when we say that they are equal."[84]

Nancy Cott's argument—that the incommensurability between men and women is not without hierarchical meaning—is useful for understanding Bushnell's views of women and men. Bushnell stated that women and men were "unlike in kind," and, therefore, were incommensurable. However, he also viewed the relationship between men and women as hierarchical. Hence, his understanding of the relationship between men and women encompassed both views, and is another example of his complexity.

In addition, Bushnell introduced another point of disagreement with women's vote, a point that came from yet another perspective.

He remarked, "The male and female natures together constitute the proper man, and are, therefore, both represented in the vote of the man."[85] That is, he believed that women were represented in their husbands' votes. He pointed out that this view corresponded with Roman or civil law, English common law, Russian law, Chinese law, and laws in other countries.[86] He noted:

> In the English common law she [a woman] is said to be *femme covert* [a married woman], a woman who is included, as respects all civil rights, in her husband. Her personality is so far merged in his, that she can not bring a suit any more in her own name, for it is a name no longer known to the law. The assumption is that, being in and of her husband, he will both act and answer for her.[87]

Again, one should note the complexity of Bushnell's argument. Elsewhere, he argued that the rights of women should be carefully defended by law from every kind of encroachment, whether by her husband or by others.[88] In this statement, he claims that married women are absorbed under their husband's names and technically have no legal rights of their own.

John Hooker, the husband of Isabella Beecher Hooker, was critical of Bushnell's attitudes. In 1879, Hooker wrote an article entitled, "Is the Family the Basis of the State?" In this article, he noted:

> What is meant by the proposition as generally used is, that the State is politically an aggregate of families and not of individuals. This is entirely untrue. . . . The first duty of the citizen is to forget that he belongs to any family particular. He is an individual citizen of the State. . . . The political basis of the state is the individual and not the family. The individual is made the voter—not the family—and that is the whole question.[89]

But, to Bushnell's way of thinking, it was not the individual but the family that was the social, political, and religious unit. In addition, he regarded the man (father or husband), not the woman (mother or wife), as the representative of the whole family. Thus, Hooker and Bushnell disagree on the basis of the social, political, and religious unit and on who represents that unit.

Furthermore, Bushnell claimed that even a woman without a husband should not have a right to vote and hold office. He believed that "the whole female order would be most effectively represented in the whole male order."[90] He concluded in the following manner:

> The sex-nature of men and women is not altered by marriage, and according to that sex-nature, women are to be sheltered legally by men. Government is not given them, but protectors are given them, who are tender above all terms of equality. . . . There is to be secured for women a more benignant, softer kind of protectorship, which is bruised and battered by no contests, or made hard and imperious by no mere dominations of force.[91]

Bushnell believed that men/husbands protected women/wives, and that women/wives were sheltered by men/husbands. However, he was unclear regarding the exact function of men's protection of women. Additionally, he expected women to embrace men in the shelter of the home, an activity that allowed women to give men a form of emotional protection from the storms of the outer world.[92]

Bushnell rejected not only women's suffrage, but also men's suffrage as an inalienable natural right. He felt that neither female nor male suffrage was related to the issue of natural rights.

Daniel Walker Howe observes that Bushnell was not at all embarrassed by his dislike of universal suffrage for both men and women, because he refused the doctrine of natural rights.[93] Robert L. Edwards concurs, adding that as "part democrat and part theocrat," Bushnell always had questions about "the inalienable natural right of suffrage even for men."[94] Edwards' comments suggest that Bushnell looked to the theocracy of the New England fathers as the basis for his arguments.[95] Paula Baker points out that political activity between men and women in the colonial era was not as obvious as in the nineteenth century. She explains that many locations required men to own property in order to be eligible to vote. Not only in the colonial period, but also into the nineteenth century, men did not always have access to the polls,[96] because property restrictions on male vote lasted into the 1820s (and even later in certain states).[97] She observes that when states began to allow men without property to vote, women finally made the connection between their non-voting status and their sex.[98]

It is not surprising, then, that Bushnell also looked to historical laws and customs to support his own argument disallowing the vote for both men and women as an inalienable right. He wrote:

> Some of us have been voting on the score of our property; some on the right we have bought by military service; some on the ground of qualifications imparted by our education; some on the count of our slaves. Doubtless we that are males are all so far equal, but we never to this day have been allowed to vote on our naked equality, except in here and there a single State. How then does it fare with the argument that women have a right, on the score of their equality with men, when men themselves cannot vote on the score of their own equality with one another?[99]

Bushnell, then, saw that property was not the only qualification for male voting eligibility, although Baker easily connected the end of the property requirement for male voting with women's awareness that sex difference had become the only thing keeping them from the polls. Bushnell, however, saw that property historically was not the only qualification for male voting eligibility. He observed that military service, education, and the number of slaves could have been regarded respectively as the eligibility in order for men to vote. His point was that historically, voting had never been a matter of inalienable natural rights.

The following question, however, emerges. A characteristic of Bushnell's way of viewing women and men was his use of the concept of nature. Therefore, to base an anti-voting argument on this notion makes the relationship between men and women absolute, fixed, and unchangeable. At the same time, Bushnell did not see voting as an issue of inalienable natural rights (which are also considered to be absolute, fixed and unchangeable.) When it came to the issue of voting, then, he used an argument based on the absolute, fixed natures of men and women, but at the same time refuted the idea of absolute and fixed rights. Once again, he reveals a degree of complexity in the structure of his thinking.

Bushnell's discussion regarding suffrage shifted next from voting to holding office. He suggested that, for a man to hold office, he should be elected by contest, rather than elected by vote. The contest method, which consists of trials of merit and personal qualification, is the West Point method. Bushnell offered the following explanation of the procedure:

> The humblest as well as the highest of the youth, are put in schooling, and then are sifted three times over, by three great examinations that go up by an ascending series. And then, out of the very limited number of the ca-

> dets that are crowned at the last, are to come all the high officers of the kingdom—officers to be who will be known as long as they live, to have excelled, first, in scholarship; secondly, in talent and capacity of writing; and thirdly, in the well-attested record of an up-right, pure behavior.[100]

The process focused on raising the brightest and best to positions of authority. This, of course, was not a democratic approach, and it is clear that it would have automatically excluded women.

Bushnell's Fears of Practical Results of Women's Suffrage

Bushnell feared a variety of ominous results if women's suffrage became a reality. He was afraid that women's bodies would change; that their emotions would become violent; that they would avoid marriage; and that they would divorce their husbands. He also feared that women would reject motherhood and that this would have a correspondingly negative effect on children. Furthermore, he worried that women would reject their very womanhood.

Bushnell used vivid images to describe the changes in women's bodies that would result if they went into the political world. Their appearance would become sharp, their voices wiry and shrill. They would become thinner, sharp-featured, lank and dry.[101]

He was fearful that suffrage would also cause an immense emotional transformation in women. He wrote:

> We shall see, when the days of women's suffrage are come, that women are a great deal more violent, constitutionally speaking, than men; the very delicacy of their nature makes them so, and as soon as they are called to violence, which now they are not, they will make an element of unmitigated bitterness. When the charities of a womanly nature are burned out, and nothing left but spleen or frenzied passion, we have a spectacle both sad and frightful.[102]

Therefore, Bushnell feared that women would become violent, bad-tempered, and frenzied—the opposite of what he understood their true nature to be.

Bushnell also observed that the hysterical excitement of a political campaign would lead women to be strained, coarse, and even violent. He explained that men did not run this risk, since their nature already possessed a certain kind of coarseness. However, he believed that women were at great risk precisely because they lacked the masculine coarseness necessary to operate in the heady political environment. In Bushnell's mind, women's exposure to politics would only lead to their becoming violent.[103]

He worried that suffrage would cause women to avoid marriage. He said, "The general scheme of women's suffrage works against marriage to make it less sacred and less permanent and just as much less beneficial."[104] This presented a problem for him, since he viewed marriage as crucial for family propagation—and family propagation was the basis of the American nation's prosperity.[105]

Bushnell was fearful that if the reform for women's suffrage was carried out, then the bonds of the family union would be loosened and women who were dissatisfied with marriage would try to obtain a divorce.[106] He thought that suffrage would bring female discontent with marriage, and then would be followed by legislation to expedite legal divorce.[107] He went on to note, "Frequent divorces check the rate of populations. Frequent divorces are the bane of all family peace and order before they come, and the extinction of all true family life and nurture after they come."[108] He also pointed out that divorce had a bad effect on children:

> Hapless beings are the children, that being heirs just now to a parentage and a home, are only heirs henceforth to a family quarrel. . . . Sad and decadent is the history of any people who have forgotten how to sanctify marriage, and whose children go to the records of divorce instead of the records of marriage, to find their fathers and mothers.[109]

However, Bushnell thought that even if divorce did not happen, women's suffrage would have a negative effect on children. In his mind, political excitement in the mother would be emotionally and physically disturbing to children during the crucial pre-natal and infancy stages of life.[110]

Additionally, he was afraid that if women were granted suffrage, then they would cease to care about their motherhood. That is, he worried that women's attention to their children would be diminished. Bushnell thought that such a response by women would be nothing short of disastrous, for he understood motherhood to be "a kind of first gospel in the flesh."[111] He noted:

> The child is born into the lap of a covert, gladly worshipful motherhood; drinks in patience, reverence, subordination, to the one idea of the family headship, and is so to be partially configured to the grand moral headship of the

> Supreme Father. And hence it is that motherhoods obtain such ineradicable, inexpugnable possession of the life of sons and daughters. Fathers have a certain power and are held in dear respect. But it is the subject nature of motherhood, the patient, self-forgetting element it makes, that fastens a feeling so deep in the child.[112]

However, he argued, if mothers went out of the home in order to be campaigners, then children would no longer be tethered to God by the presence of a nearly divine form of motherhood.[113]

Furthermore, Bushnell feared that if women's suffrage reform became reality, then women would reject womanhood altogether. He observed that discontented women seemed to be quarreling with their womanhood, seeking to emulate masculine spheres, and aspiring to masculine offices.[114] He, therefore, advised women to maintain their womanhood and not to compete with men, because he acknowledged womanhood as "the most honorable, finest, highest nature."[115]

Bushnell's Design for Women's Participation in Politics

Bushnell rejected the idea of women directing political affairs. However, as a compromise, he offered a blueprint for their participation in politics. He suggested the following:

> A reconstruction of our government is conceivable. . . . If there were a second or third house, called the House of Women, interposed between our Senate and Representative chambers, in such a way that any measure could originate in either, and every measure must pass the vote of the three, this would give full opportunity to the women to look after their own affairs, and after all fit legislations by which they may best advance their condition.[116]

Bushnell's blueprint would have allowed women to have an effect on decisions relating to political affairs. However, he immediately realized that his plan would contradict the notion of the subordination of women. He added that the House of Women "would give them a legislative power, when it really does not belong to their womanly nature to govern, and would also give them a practical veto over all the governing rights of men."[117] Thus it is clear that, in Bushnell's mind, the ideal would be to separate women entirely from politics.

Bushnell's Expectation of Women for a Christian America

Although Bushnell rejected women's participation in the political world, he expected them to support his goal of a Christian America in a different way—by increasing the American population through marriage and childbirth, and by using Christian values and principles to nurture children. Despite this opinion, he did not want to force women to stay at home. Previous scholars have used Horace Bushnell to represent Americans who believed that women's sphere was limited to the home. However, in actuality, Bushnell did not deny women the opportunity to participate in outside activities. It was women's suffrage, per se, that he disagreed with. He also expected women to help build a Christian America by preaching and functioning as deaconesses in the church. One of the main reasons that Bushnell opposed women's suffrage was that he believed the movement threatened to disturb the Christianization of America, for which, in Bushnell's mind, male ministers had labored for a century.

Responses to Bushnell's Views on Women's Suffrage

Bushnell's contemporaries had various reactions to his views on women's suffrage. William James, in his review of Bushnell's *Women's Suffrage; The Reform Against Nature* in *North American Review* in 1869, attempted to connect Bushnell with Catholicism and seemed to be questioning the Hartford minister's attachment to Protestantism. James stated:

> Her [Woman's] supreme glory is to be a "subject nature . . . milder, truer, and closer to the type of God's own dear submissions in the cross of his Son," than our "coarse forbidding masculinities" will let us attain. This is nothing but the good old Catholic doctrine, invented when people were hopeless of an order to be realized in this world, that suffering is a higher vocation than action.[118]

Orestes A. Brownson, a convert to Roman Catholicism, wrote two articles related to women's issues: "The Woman Question, Article I" in 1869 and "The Woman Question, Article II" in 1873.[119] In "The Woman Question, Article II," Brownson reviewed Bushnell's *Women's Suffrage; The Reform Against Nature* and noted that he and Bushnell were of like minds on the issue:

> We are happy to find that Dr. Bushnell, the distinguished author of the first of the two works we have placed at the head of this article [*Women's Suffrage; The Reform Against Nature* by Horace Bushnell and *The Woman Who Dared* by Epes Sargent], fully agrees with us.[120]

As did Bushnell, Brownson questioned the notion that voting was a natural right. He wrote:

> We agree entirely with the American congress [Congress] of 1776, when they say they hold as self-evident that "all men are created equal" and are "endowed with certain inalienable rights, among which are life, liberty, and the pursuit of happiness;" but when they say that "all just governments derive their powers from the consent of the governed," we do by no means accept their dictum, for reasons which we gave in the article on the *Democratic Principle*. We, therefore, do not admit that either suffrage or eligibility, the right to vote or to be voted for, is a natural right for either man or woman.[121]

However, the two men parted company on at least one important issue. Brownson regarded all men and women as created equal. Bushnell, on the other hand, believed that women were created to be the "meet-helpers" of men—that is, that they were created to be subsidiary to men.

Brownson, further, explained that suffrage was not a natural right, but a civil or political right.[122] Although Bushnell did not consider suffrage to be a natural right, he did not say whether or not he believed suffrage was a civil and/or political right.[123]

Isabella Beecher Hooker also responded to Bushnell's *Women's Suffrage; The Reform Against Nature*. Her critique, however, was anything but favorable. Robert L. Edwards comments that Hooker wrote scathingly critical comments all over the book's margins, "such as, 'Try it, dear friend, you will never touch bottom till you leap,' 'shameful,' or 'utterly false.'"[124]

John Hooker, the husband of Isabella Beecher Hooker, was critical as well, writing in the January 17, 1871 edition of the *Evening Post*:

> One noble woman . . . said to me [Hooker], on reading Dr. Bushnell's remark in his book on woman suffrage, that these women were only trying to make themselves men: "Cruel, cruel words! If so noble a man as Dr.

> Bushnell so utterly fails to comprehend a woman's nature, shall not she be allowed to speak for herself, and no testimony be taken but hers?"[125]

Contemporary scholar Ronald William Hogeland notes, "Bushnell saw the suffrage movement largely in terms of women desiring to become like men by sacrificing their finer natures for power and position."[126] Hogeland also remarks that Bushnell's purpose was not to preserve the world of masculinity, but to protect women from the corruption of political life.[127] Indeed, Horace Bushnell regarded the political world of his era as corrupt; therefore he sought to protect women from that corruption. However, Hogeland's comment that Bushnell's purpose was not to preserve the world of masculinity does not seem quite accurate. Clearly, Bushnell was trying to preserve the world of male dominance by arguing that men's nature was to govern women, and that women's nature was to be subordinate to men.

Conrad Cherry offers an explanation of why Bushnell took a stand against women's suffrage:

> Nature revealed no flexibility when Bushnell appealed to its structures in his discussions of race and sex. . . . The lamentation applies to Bushnell's own views of nature. It was as if, in expelling the mechanistic nature of the Enlightenment, he had thrust himself into a natural mechanism even more rigid in his opinions of blacks and women, unable or unwilling fully to grasp the truth of his flexible cosmos.[128]

Cherry's comments make a great deal of sense. Bushnell's views of nature—the natures of women and men in this case—did indeed lack flexibility and were rigid. According to Cherry, such an understanding of male and female natures would not and could not, endorse the notion of women's suffrage.

Bushnell's Ideological Limitations

Steven M. Buechler offers three distinct ideological traditions of the women's suffrage movement in nineteenth-century America, based on work done by Olive Banks.[129] The first tradition is that of evangelical Christianity, which emphasized women's moral superiority.[130] In reality, though, this tradition was inclined to promote "a more oppositional feminist stance."[131] The second ideological tradition is that of the Enlightenment, which stressed natural rights, liberal individualism, and sexual equality.[132] The third tradition is that of socialist feminism, which underscored "secular and communal values in contradistinction to the religiosity of evangelical Christianity and the individualism of Enlightenment philosophy."[133] Buechler believes that the demand for women's suffrage in nineteenth-century America included all three ideological traditions.

Buechler's analysis of the women's suffrage movement in nineteenth-century America makes it clear that Bushnell's polemics focused mainly on the Enlightenment tradition, from the viewpoint of evangelical Christianity based on the emphasis of women's religious superiority. In other words, he argued against the Enlightenment tradition of the women's suffrage movement by employing the same arguments used by evangelical Christianity that, in actuality, promoted an anti-suffrage movement. He also did not respond to the socialist feminism tradition of the women's suffrage movement. Thus, his views on the suffrage movement did not take in the full scope of the issue, but had ideological limitations.

Women's Sphere in Society

Except for the political field, Bushnell believed that women's sphere should be expanded in society. In addition, he believed that female and male spheres should not necessarily be sharply separate. Rather, he thought that the two spheres could be combined with each other.

Bushnell's Disagreement with the Paradigm of Separate Spheres

Linda K. Kerber explains that in the 1960s, historians Barbara Welter, Aileen S. Kraditor, and Gerda Lerner highlighted the importance of the "separate spheres" metaphor to nineteenth-century Americans.[134] The spheres supposedly inhabited by men and by women are succinctly described by David G. Hackett:

> "Women's sphere" describes a female-dominated household world of piety and domesticity. Emerging with the separation of the workplace from the home in the early nineteenth century, the ideology of separate spheres held to a dichotomized view of male and female nature whereby men occupied a public sphere of economics and politics while women held sway over a private sphere of children, religion, and morality.[135]

Hackett's definition may have adequately described a nineteenth-century paradigm, but it is not the same as Bushnell's views of the two spheres.

For example, in *Christian Nurture* it seems that Bushnell advised men to participate equally with women in nurturing children. In addition, in *Women's Suffrage; The Reform Against Nature* he encouraged women to embrace the possibilities of employment outside the home much more than some scholars imagine. In reality, Bushnell accepted and supported the idea of women working outside. He did not insist that women's sphere should be limited to their homes, as most scholars note, even though he regarded the home as a crucial aspect of the female sphere.

Bushnell's Observation about the Condition of Women

Bushnell confessed, "If I were a woman, in the present lot of women, I think I should certainly wish to be a man."[136] In addition, he admitted, "We are surprised to find how many disadvantages are laid upon the condition of woman that no principle of equity permits, and no pretense of reason or necessity justifies."[137] The disadvantages he listed were many: the property rights of men and women were not equal; the redress of their personal wrongs was unequal; women's employment was restricted; wages were not equal; and women did not have the "counter force" to resist their subjection to "an overbearing tyrant."[138] Bushnell also was of the opinion that employment needed to be based on qualifications, and that wages ought to be decided on the basis of a woman's ability and personality, including her physical appearance and voice.[139]

Women's Sphere in Society

To improve the condition of women, Bushnell first of all supported a co-educational system.[140] He believed that women who were educated with men would be able to become educators with men,[141] or professors of languages, botany, moral sciences, and mathematics. However, he was not of the opinion that women ought to be professors in disciplines such as mechanical philosophy, chemistry, metallurgy, or fortification, although he did not explain why these disciplines were not suitable.[142] At the same time, he regarded the profession of medicine to be appropriate for both women and men. Bushnell, furthermore, endorsed women's participation in the legal profession. He also acknowledged that women such as Harriet Beecher Stowe, Margaret Fuller,[143] and Gail Hamilton had gained advantages in the fields of art and literary production.[144] Bushnell predicted that women's business ability would be more respected in the future and anticipated that they would have occupations in the trades and hotel management, and would work as bank-tellers, brokers, actuaries of insurance companies, private bankers, type-setters, and overseers of printing.[145]

Bushnell also encouraged women to go into arenas such as almshouses and hospitals. He felt that these spheres should be part of "the mercies and benignities, and faithful charities of private life, and particularly the private life of women."[146] It is significant that he understood charity to be an important way of life. As discussed in Chapters 2 and 3, he tried to open his daughters' eyes to the less fortunate and urged them to be merciful. He greatly respected the work of his parishioner, Mary Lyman Collins, who engaged in acts of charity, and he also regarded the role of deaconess as important.

In addition, Bushnell suggested that women should teach in the common school, and offered the following reasons:

> We have certain benefits from our common schools, but we are coming down rapidly now upon the fact, that no religion can be taught, and not even a religious morality, because it will infringe on some misbelief, or variant belief; and the charge that was laid by the Catholic is becoming more painfully [painful] just every year.[147]

Hence, Bushnell wanted women to become common school teachers because the schools were not teaching religion. In his opinion, religious education in the common school needed to be taught by women, the cultural carriers of religion. He believed that women, rather than men, were the bearers of religion because women's religious nature was superior to men. Of course, by "religion," Bushnell meant a general type of Christianity that included both Protestantism and Catholicism. He hoped America would become essentially Christian, noting, "Common schools are to be Christian schools. Catholics and Protestants are Christians. Our government is Christian."[148] He, further, understood that 'religion' was a form of Christianity capable of uniting the American nation. According to Bushnell, if Christianity was thriving as a unified religion, then the American nation would thrive, as well.

Bushnell also believed that various ministries should be open to women. They could become preachers or deaconesses. However, as noted previously, he was not of the opinion that women should be admitted to the "official right of administration" in the church.[149]

Finally, Bushnell raised this question: "Are we called to give women an equal place with men on the ballot, and the right of public office?"[150] His answer, of course, was to reject totally both women's voting and women's office-holding. He firmly contended that once women had access to the polls, they eventually would gain the right to hold office; and the resulting situation would be the end of "the new-born, more beneficent American civilization."[151] In short, he was afraid that the American nation, itself, would wilt if women gained the right to vote and hold office.

Robert L. Edwards observes that with the exception of suffrage, "Bushnell had moments when he was a surprisingly unapologetic advocate of women's rights."[152] In truth, Bushnell supported co-education, equal wages, and the right of women to own property after marriage. Thus, he could be viewed as egalitarian. At the same time, though, he resolutely disagreed that the political sphere should be open to women; therefore, he should be seen as a separatist.

Summary of This Chapter

In this chapter, I have argued that in Bushnell's view, women's participation in politics through women's suffrage would weaken the foundations of the family, the church and nation, and lead to the decline of a Christian America based on the organic unity of family, church, and nation. However, except for the presence of women in the political field, Bushnell believed that women's place in society needed to be expanded. Thus, his thought continued to be complex even regarding issues of women's sphere in society.

Notes

[1] Horace Bushnell, *The Fathers of New England*, (New York: Geo. P. Putnam, 1850), 43.

[2] For the basis of my opinion, see "New England Fathers and Revolutionary Fathers" in this chapter.

[3] Daniel Walker Howe points out that Bushnell considered family, religious bodies, and nations to be organic communities. See Daniel Walker Howe, "The Social Science of Horace Bushnell," *The Journal of American History* 70, no. 2 (September 1983): 316.

[4] Horace Bushnell, *Christian Nurture* (New York: Charles Scribner, 1861; reprint, Grand Rapids: Baker Book House, 1979), 406.

[5] Ibid., 314.

[6] Horace Bushnell, *Crisis of the Church* (Hartford: Daniel Burgess and Co., 1835), 11. This is a sermon delivered by Bushnell at his North Congregational Church in 1835, and published that same year. This sermon is the first of his many publications.

[7] Horace Bushnell, *Reverses Needed* (Hartford: L.E. Hunt, 1861), 15. Bushnell delivered this discourse to his own congregation on the Sunday just after the disaster of the first battle of Bull Run in July, 1861.

[8] Horace Bushnell, "The True Wealth or Weal of Nations," in *Work and Play* (New York: Charles Scribner, 1864), 66. Bushnell delivered this oration before the Society of Phi Beta Kappa, Yale College, on August 15, 1837.

[9] Horace Bushnell, "American Politics," *The American National Preacher* 14 (December 1840): 203-04. Bushnell wrote this sermon before the national election of 1840.

[10] Bushnell, *Christian Nurture*, 406.

[11] Ibid., 63.

[12] Howe, "The Social Science of Horace Bushnell," 308.

[13] Bushnell also viewed individualism from another perspective. He noted that the culture's over-emphasis on individualism and the self tended to harden people emotionally. See Bushnell, *Christian Nurture*, 219.

This perspective is important when one investigates Bushnell's view of women and men. He believed that the type of individualism mentioned above caused the loss of womanhood and/or motherhood.

[14] Bushnell, *Christian Nurture*, 91.

[15] Mary Bushnell Cheney, ed., *Life and Letters of Horace Bushnell* (New York: Harper & Brothers, Publishers, 1880; reprint, New York: Arno Press & *The New York Times*, 1969), 178.

[16] David L. Smith, ed., *Horace Bushnell: Selected Writings on Language, Religion, and American Culture* (Chico: Scholars Press, 1984), 151.

[17] Ibid., 151.

[18] Bushnell, *Christian Nurture*, 195.

[19] Ibid., 200.

[20] Horace Bushnell, "The Doctrine of Loyalty," in *Work and Play* (New York: Charles Scribner, 1864), 344. The first publication of this article appeared in July, 1863, in volume XXII of *The New Englander.* Conrad Cherry, in particular, regards Bushnell's notion of loyalty as crucial to his concept of the American nation. Cherry notes: "The key to Bushnell's organic conception of the nation is his doctrine of loyalty. That doctrine is his way of affirming the unity and basic sentiment of a nationality that underlies and is prior to particular laws, constitutions, states and other parts of the whole." See Conrad Cherry, "The Structure of Organic Thinking: Horace Bushnell's Approach to Language, Nature, and Nation," *Journal of the American Academy of Religion* 40 (1972): 14.

[21] Bushnell, "The Doctrine of Loyalty," 358.

[22] Horace Bushnell, *Barbarism the First Danger* (New York: The American Home Missionary Society, 1847), 32. This address was delivered in New York, Boston, and other places in May and June, 1847. This was Bushnell's first public address, for which he became widely known.

[23] Bushnell, *The Fathers of New England*, 42.

[24] Regarding a monarchy, see "New England Fathers and Revolutionary Fathers" in this chapter.

[25] In addition, Bushnell preferred the American doctrine of federal rights to the state-rights doctrine derived from John Calhoun.

[26] Howard A. Barnes, *Horace Bushnell and the Virtuous Republic* (Metuchen: The Scarecrow Press, Inc., 1991), 47.

[27] Barnes, 47. David Alan Jones notes, "Horace Bushnell was no activist. He was a preacher, an intellectual, and a moralist. Although he was intensely concerned about public affairs, his own participation remained on an intellectual level." See David Alan Jones, "The Social and Political Thought of Horace Bushnell: An Interpretation of the Mid-Nineteenth-Century American Mind" (Ph.D. diss., Northwestern University, Evanston, 1973), 46. Daniel Walker Howe points out that Bushnell's political thought resembles that of the Whig party (roughly, 1834-54). See Howe, "The Social Science of Horace Bushnell," 308. Paula Baker notes, "A national two-party system rose in the 1820s and 1830s." See Paula Baker, "The Domestication of Politics: Women and American Political Society, 1780-1920," *American Historical Review* 89 (1984): 627. During Bushnell's time, there were more than two parties at large in America. Moreover, the conditions of those political parties were complex.

[28] Daniel Walker Howe categorizes the New England fathers and the Revolutionary fathers as Puritanism and the continental Enlightenment respectively. See Daniel Walker Howe, *The Political Culture of the American Whigs* (Chicago and London: The University of Chicago Press, 1979), 69. James H. Moorhead states, "The genesis of the United States could not be located at Philadelphia in 1776; the nation was contained in embryo among the first New England settlers." James H. Moorhead, *American Apocalypse: Yankee Protestants and the Civil War, 1860-1869* (New Haven and London: Yale University Press, 1978), 140.

[29] Robert L. Edwards, *Of Singular Genius, Of Singular Grace: A Biography of Horace Bushnell* (Cleveland: The Pilgrim Press, 1992), 228.

[30] Horace Bushnell, *Popular Government by Divine Right* (Hartford: L.E. Hunt, 1864), 12. Bushnell delivered this sermon before the congregations of the South Church and the South Baptist Church, Hartford, on the day of the national Thanksgiving, 24 November 1864.

[31] Benedict Anderson points out: "It is instructive that the Declaration of Independence in 1776 speaks only of 'the people,' while the word 'nation' makes its debut only in the Constitution of 1789." Furthermore, Anderson adds, "The Declaration of Independence of 1776 makes absolutely no reference to the Pilgrim fathers, nor are the grounds put forward to justify independence in any way 'historical,' in the sense of highlighting the antiquity of the American people. Indeed, marvelously, the American nation is not even mentioned. A profound feeling that a radical break with the past was occurring—a 'blasting open of the continuum of history'?—spread rapidly." See Benedict Anderson, *Imagined Communities: Reflections on the Origin and Spread of Nationalism* (New York: Verso, 1991), 65, 193.

[32] The "editor's preface" of *Moral Uses of Dark Things* points out that "the strength of his [Bushnell's] own hereditary Puritan consciousness is revealed" in *The Fathers of New England*. Horace Bushnell, *Moral Uses of Dark Things* (New York: Charles Scribner & Co., 1868), iv. Mary Cheney states, "His [Bushnell's] filial sentiment of obligation to the Puritan fathers of New England flowered here [in *The Fathers of New England*] in a lofty tribute." See Cheney, ed., 229.

[33] Bushnell, *The Fathers of New England*, 26. Bushnell also noted, "They [The New England fathers] were all, to a man, royalists and true Englishmen—pleased with the hope of 'endeavoring the advancement of his Majesty's dominion.'" Ibid., 23.

[34] Ibid., 14, 19.

[35] Bushnell, *The Fathers of New England*, 42. In another place, Bushnell said, "They [The New England fathers] stood for God and religion alone. . . . They believed in the Bible, and in God's decrees, and they came over to profess the one and fulfil the other." Ibid., 39.

[36] Bushnell, *Reverses Needed*, 10.

[37] Bushnell, *The Fathers of New England*, 23. In another work, Bushnell commented, "Our nation stood to represent the principle of Self-Government. In the very birth of its independence, it overthrew partly as the accident and partly as the proper effect of that event, one of the most ancient and established monarchies of Europe." This appeared to frustrate him. Bushnell, *Crisis of the Church*, 7.

[38] Bushnell, *The Fathers of New England*, 24. Bushnell also said that the New England fathers acknowledged the king as the rightful head of the church. Ibid., 24.

[39] Bushnell, *Popular Government by Divine Right*, 4.

[40] According to Bushnell, the other two crises in the history of the American nation were the State Rights doctrine of John Caldwell Calhoun and the Civil War. See Bushnell, *Popular Government by Divine Right*, 4-16.

[41] Bushnell, *Reverses Needed,* 11.

[42] Bushnell, *Popular Government by Divine* Right, 5. Bushnell also noted that American leadership had been greatly influenced by French political theorists, like Rousseau. Bushnell explained that these writers "began at the point of what they called nature and natural right in men, contriving how civil society might arise, and could only lawfully, by their consent, or compact, or vote, and the surrender of their individual rights, to make up the public stock of powers and prerogatives in the state." Bushnell added that other influences on leaders were found in American churches, as well as town and colonial democracies. Bushnell explained, "As a natural result, the two schools flowed together, coalescing in the same declarations of right." Ibid., 4-5.

[43] Bushnell, *Reverses Needed,* 13.

[44] This is Bushnell's interpretation. Before the Revolutionary era, the nation had not actually been established.

[45] Elizabeth Cady Stanton, Susan B. Anthony, and Matilda Joslyn Gage, eds., *History of Woman Suffrage* Vol. I (Rochester: Charles Mann, 1887), 68.

[46] Harry L. Watson, *Liberty and Power: The Politics of Jacksonian America* (New York: Hill and Wang, 1989), 13.

[47] Elizabeth Cady Stanton, Susan B. Anthony, and Matilda Joslyn Gage, eds., *History of Woman Suffrage* Vol. I, 67.

[48] Ibid., 70-71.

[49] Susan E. Marshall, *Splintered Sisterhood: Gender and Class in the Campaign against Woman Suffrage* (Madison: The University of Wisconsin Press, 1997), 18.

[50] Ibid., 19-20. Barbara Welter notes that the 1871 petition was signed "by Mrs. General Sherman, Mrs. Admiral Dahlgren and One Thousand Ladies . . . ." See Barbara Welter , "Something Remains to Dare: Introduction to *The Woman's Bible*," in *The Original Feminist Attack on the Bible*, by Elizabeth Cady Stanton et al. (Reprint, New York: Arno Press, 1974), xv.

[51] Marshall, 20. According to the original petition which was appeared in the editorial pages of *Godey's Lady's Book and Magazine*, the petitioners gave the following reasons for signing the documents: "Because Holy Scripture inculcates a different, and for us higher sphere, apart from public life. Because as women, we find a full measure of duties, cares, and responsibilities devolving upon us, and we are therefore unwilling to bear other and heavier burdens and those unsuited to our physical organization. Because we hold that an extension of suffrage would be adverse to the interest of the working women of the country, with whom we heartily sympathize. Because these changes must introduce a fruitful element of discord in the existing marriage relation, which would tend to the infinite detriment of children, and increase the already alarming prevalence of divorce throughout the land. Because general law, affecting the condition of all women, should be framed to meet exceptional discontent. "Editors' Table," *Godey's Lady's Book and Magazine*, 491 (May 1871): 476.

[52] Marshall, 19.

[53] Elizabeth Cady Stanton, Susan B. Anthony, and Matilda Joslyn Gage, eds., *History of Woman Suffrage* Vol. III (Rochester: Charles Mann, 1887), 317.

[54] Carole Nichols, *Votes and More for Women: Suffrage and After in Connecticut* (New York: The Institutes for Research in History and The Haworth Press, Inc., 1983), 6. According to Nichols, "Isabella Beecher Hooker dominated the struggle for women's rights in Connecticut during the last three decades of the nineteenth century." Ibid., 6. In addition, Nichols notes, "Frances Ellen Burr, a lecturer and writer, made pioneering efforts to win the

franchise in Connecticut." Ibid., 5. Furthermore, Nichols writes, "Burr later was part of a group of twenty-three women comprising the 'Revising Committee' which published Part I of the *Woman's Bible* in 1895." Ibid., 56.

55 Nichols, 6.

56 Ibid., 56. Clifford E. Clark, Jr., *Henry Ward Beecher: Spokesman for a Middle-Class American* (Chicago: University of Illinois Press, 1978), 206. Clark, Jr. uses the term, "conservative."

57 Clark, 198.

58 Marshall, 20.

59 Clark, Jr., 206.

60 Nichols, 6-7.

61 Ibid., 5.

62 Clark, Jr., 202.

63 Horace Bushnell, *Women's Suffrage; The Reform Against Nature* (New York: Charles Scribner and Company, 1869), 100-01. This matter is discussed later in this chapter.

64 Elizabeth Cady Stanton, Susan B. Anthony, and Matilda Joslyn Gage, eds., *History of Woman Suffrage* Vol. III, 317-18.

65 Bushnell, "American Politics," 189-204. Ronald William Hogeland also points out, "The consistency of Bushnell's view upon this subject [women's suffrage] can be seen by reading his initial published essay, "American Politics," in 1840 and his *Women's Suffrage* which incorporates essentially his earlier views." See Ronald Hogeland, "Femininity and the Nineteenth Century Post-Puritan Mind" (Ph.D. diss., University of California, Los Angeles, 1968), 165.

66 Bushnell, "American Politics," 199.

67 Bushnell, *Women's Suffrage; The Reform Against Nature*, 105.

68 Ibid., 74.

[69] Bushnell, *Women's Suffrage; The Reform Against Nature*, 105.

[70] Ibid., 107.

[71] Ibid., 109.

[72] Ibid., 109.

[73] Ibid., 100-01. This is not Henry Ward Beecher's paragraph itself, but is paraphrased by Bushnell. Henry Ward Beecher's actual quote comes from the speech, "Woman Suffrage Man's Right," given at the Cooper Institute in 1860. "If God made woman with a genius of refinement, tenderness, and moral purity, it is not probable that the exercise of large public duty will efface the marks of her original constitution, and that an active patriotism will tarnish her purity, and that zeal for public justice will demoralize her nature." See Halford R. Ryan, *Henry Ward Beecher: Peripatetic Preacher* (New York: Greenwood Press, 1990), 105.

[74] Bushnell, *Women's Suffrage; The Reform Against Nature*, 101.

[75] Ibid., 102.

[76] Ibid., 103.

[77] Ibid., 104.

[78] Ibid., 106.

[79] Ibid., 106.

[80] Ibid., 35.

[81] Ibid., 37-38.

[82] Ibid., 36.

[83] Bushnell, *Women's Suffrage; The Reform Against Nature*, 35-37. In addition, Bushnell cited the *Nation*, a journal with which he agreed. He claimed that the difference between the sexes was "radical and essential." Bushnell said that men and women were not only physically different, but also unlike mentally and morally. He wrote: "They neither think, feel, wish, purpose, will, nor act alike. They take the same views of nothing. The old statements that one is passive, the other active; one emotional, the other moral; one affectionate, the other rational; one sentimental, the other intellectual, are likely

to be more than verified by science. . . . That both [men and women] can not occupy the same place, do the same work, or reach the same standard, ought to be assumed. Nature has decreed it so." Ibid., 36-37.

[84] Bushnell, *Women's Suffrage; The Reform Against Nature*, 37.

[85] Ibid., 67.

[86] The view that women should be represented in their husbands' votes corresponds to the old Japanese law, too.

[87] Bushnell, *Women's Suffrage; The Reform Against Nature*, 68.

[88] Ibid., 28-29.

[89] Elizabeth Cady Stanton, Susan B. Anthony, and Matilda Joslyn Gage, eds., *History of Woman Suffrage* Vol. III, 958.

[90] Bushnell, *Women's Suffrage; The Reform Against Nature*, 71.

[91] Ibid., 71.

[92] This was discussed in the "Women in the Family" chapter.

[93] Howe, "The Social Science of Horace Bushnell," 319.

[94] Edwards, *Of Singular Genius, Of Singular Grace*, 263.

[95] About the theocracy of the New England fathers, see "New England Fathers and Revolutionary Fathers" in this chapter.

[96] Baker, 623.

[97] Ibid., 625.

[98] Ibid., 629.

[99] Bushnell, *Women's Suffrage; The Reform Against Nature*, 39. See also Ibid., 42.

[100] Ibid., 46.

[101] Bushnell, *Women's Suffrage; The Reform Against Nature*, 135-36. Compare this description with that of Bushnell's mother's appearance as his ideal woman, as noted in Chapter 2.

[102] Ibid., 132-33. In another place, Bushnell pointed out that if women's suffrage became a reality, then only women's selfishness, barbarism, and aridity would be left. Ibid., 161.

[103] Ibid., 140.

[104] Ibid., 156.

[105] See also Chapter 2.

[106] Bushnell, *Women's Suffrage; The Reform Against Nature*, 152, 154.

[107] Ibid., 155.

[108] Ibid., 156.

[109] Ibid., 156-57.

[110] Ibid., 152.

[111] Ibid., 171.

[112] Ibid., 171.

[113] Ibid., 171-72.

[114] Ibid., 170.

[115] Ibid., 170.

[116] Ibid., 151.

[117] Ibid., 152.

[118] William James, "Bushnell's Women's Suffrage," *The North American Review* 109 (October 1869): 557-58.

[119] Barbara Welter provides a fine summary of Brownson's views of women in a footnote to her article, "The Feminization of American Religion." Welter

notes, "He [Brownson] saw the weakening of American family life as the greatest crisis of the age, and the women's movement, in its stress on individual rights, hastened the dissolution of the family as a social unit and contributed to the disastrous trend of isolation." See Barbara Welter, "The Feminization of American Religion: 1800-1860," in *Dimity Convictions: The American Woman in the Nineteenth Century* (Athens: Ohio University Press, 1976), 221.

[120] Orestes A. Brownson, "The Woman Question, Article II," in *The Works of Orestes A. Brownson* vol. XVIII, ed. Henry F. Brownson (New York: AMS Press, Inc., 1966), 401.

[121] Ibid., 401.

[122] Ibid., 401.

[123] Although Orestes Brownson agreed with Bushnell's views of women and women's suffrage, Brownson firmly disagreed with Bushnell's *God in Christ* published in 1849. Robert L. Edwards notes, "Orestes Brownson, once a Unitarian, but by this time a zealous Roman Catholic, depicted Bushnell as 'a very ignorant man' who was 'mentally and morally in a chaotic state'—'a bad theologian, but unhappily a worse philosopher'." See Edwards, *Of Singular Genius, Of Singular Grace*, 116.

[124] Ibid., 266.

[125] Elizabeth Cady Stanton, Susan B. Anthony, and Matilda Joslyn Gage, eds., *History of Woman Suffrage* Vol. III, 328.

[126] Hogeland, 166.

[127] Hogeland, 172.

[128] Conrad Cherry, *Nature and Religious Imagination: From Edwards to Bushnell* (Philadelphia: Fortress, 1980), 203.

[129] Steven M. Buechler, *Women's Movements in the United States: Woman Suffrage, Equal Rights, and Beyond* (New Brunswick and London: Rutgers University Press, 1990), 88. See also Olive Banks, *Faces of Feminism: A Study of Feminism as a Social Movement* (Cambridge: Basil Blackwell, 1981), 7-8.

[130] Buechler, 88.

[131] Buechler, 88.

[132] Ibid., 88.

[133] Ibid., 88.

[134] Linda K. Kerber, "Separate Spheres, Female Worlds, Woman's Place: The Rhetoric of Women's History," *The Journal of American History* 75, no. 1 (June 1988): 11.

[135] David G. Hackett, "Gender and Religion in American Culture, 1870-1930," *Religion and American Culture* 5, no. 2 (Summer 1995): 128-29. In addition, Hackett comments, "The origins of the dominant paradigm for American women's history is most often traced to the works of Barbara Welter, Carroll Smith-Rosenberg, Kathryn Kish Sklar, Nancy Cott, and Mary Ryan." Ibid., 128.

[136] Bushnell, *Women's Suffrage; The Reform Against Nature*, 90.

[137] Ibid., 10.

[138] Ibid., 90.

[139] Ibid., 18. Bushnell continued to be interested in woman's appearance and voice throughout his life.

[140] Bushnell's support of coeducation was influenced by Charles G. Finney. Edwards, *Of Singular Genius, Of Singular Grace,* 165.

[141] As I noted in Chapter 2, two of Bushnell's daughters were teachers.

[142] Bushnell, *Women's Suffrage; The Reform Against Nature*, 18.

[143] Why Bushnell chose Margaret Fuller raises a question. Bushnell's views of women's issues did not coincide with Fuller's progressive tendency regarding these issues. For example, Fuller endorsed women's suffrage, although implicitly. (When the women's rights movement began in America, Fuller was in Italy). See Susan Hill Lindley, *"You Have Stept Out Of Your Place": A History of Women and Religion in America* (Louiseville: Westminster John Knox Press, 1996), 284-85.

[144] Bushnell, *Women's Suffrage; The Reform Against Nature*, 26. According to Robert L. Edwards, Gail Hamilton is "Mary Abigail Dodge, a journalist

who once worked as a reporter in Hartford." Edwards, *Of Singular Genius, Of Singular Grace*, 262.

[145] Bushnell, *Women's Suffrage; The Reform Against Nature*, 27.

[146] Ibid., 179.

[147] Ibid., 181.

[148] Horace Bushnell, "Common Schools," in *Building Eras in Religion* (New York: Charles Scribner's Sons, 1881), 88-89. This discourse was delivered in the North Congregational Church, Hartford, as a Fast Day Discourse, on March 25, 1853. Bushnell's attitudes toward Catholicism are complex. It is true that he was critical of Catholicism. Yet, as one can see from the quotation, he included not only Protestantism but also Catholicism in Christianity. See also the section of "Christian America" in this chapter. In addition, Mark Edwards used the phrase, "a pioneering ecumenist, Bushnell" in a recent article. See Mark Edwards, "'My God and My Good Mother': The Irony of Horace Bushnell's Gendered Republic," *Religion and American Culture: A Journal of Interpretation* 13, no. 1 (Winter 2003): 111.

[149] See discussion in Chapter 3. Bushnell, *Women's Suffrage; The Reform Against Nature*, 25.

[150] Ibid., 29.

[151] Ibid., 31. Citing the article, "Is There Such a Thing as Sex?" written by O. B. Frothingham, Bushnell disagreed with Frothingham's idea regarding women's suffrage. Bushnell said, "It is amazing that so many of our writers and debaters are able to handle this question [women's suffrage] so lightly." Ibid., 30.

In reality, Frothingham wrote, "We do not regret the movement towards universal suffrage. We do not deprecate the experiment of it. . . . At present it is an experiment, and a crude one." See O. B. Frothingham, "Is There Such a Thing as Sex?," *The Nation* 8 (January-June 1869): 87-89.

[152] Edwards, *Of Singular Genius, Of Singular Grace*, 261.

CHAPTER 5
CONCLUSION

Summary of This Book

Horace Bushnell envisioned a Christian America based on the organic unity of family, church, and nation. A Christian America was, for him, a nation that endorsed basic Christian beliefs. He believed that the Christian religion could lead America. He also understood the institutions of family, church, and nation to be organic, and to be the cornerstones in forming, maintaining, and expanding a Christian America. Bushnell thought that his vision of a Christian America could be realized by emphasizing the importance of men's "government" of women and women's "subordination" to men. He asserted that men, by nature, should have the "governmental" function, while women should carry the "subordinate" function. His views about women were, therefore, generally patriarchal and hierarchical. However, in certain circumstances, his views regarding women were egalitarian and nurturing. Consequently, his views on women were complex.

Bushnell believed that the institution of the family—as well as those of church and nation—was a cornerstone in the construction of a Christian America. Therefore, he viewed marriage (the foundation of the family) as important. In his mind, the marriage relationship allowed men to actualize their governing nature and women to actualize their subordinate nature. Bushnell thought that through the actualization of the natures of men and women in marriage, the foundation of the family would be solid. This would then enable the nation to become strong as well. Thus, his views on marriage then did not portray an egalitarian partnership, but a protective-subordinate headship structure.

Bushnell thought that the nurture of children, particularly the nurture of children from the perspective of the parents' Christian values, was crucial to the stability and prosperity of the American family, church, and nation. Most scholars have suggested that Bushnell placed overwhelming importance on the mother as the provider of Christian nurture within the family. However, in *Christian Nurture*, Bushnell regarded the opportunities and responsibilities of both fathers and mothers as almost equal. In the cases of family prayer and family government, he even placed much more importance on fatherhood than on motherhood. His understanding of both parents' roles in the family's Christian nurture corresponds with his desire to form a solid family through the reinforcement of hierarchically complementary roles of men and women.

Even though Bushnell championed an ideal family built on men's government of women and women's subordination to men, he did not try to realize this ideal in his own family life. His relationships with his immediate family were not those of government, but rather those of equality and cooperation with his wife, and nurture with his daughters. Bushnell's correspondence with his wife does not indicate that he expected her to be subordinate to him. Based on his letters, then, it is clear that Bushnell wished to grow hand in hand, as a husband and a father, with his wife, and did not seek to govern her.

Additionally, Bushnell's letters reveal that he did not ask his daughters to be subject to him. Instead, his correspondence encouraged them to grow into intellectually and religiously cultivated women. Thus, his attitudes regarding women were egalitarian and nurturing in his immediate family. In this sense, Bushnell's views of women in the family reflected a complexity between his ideal notion and his actual practice of family life.

Bushnell highly valued women's religious nature and regarded it as superior to that of men. He believed that women's religious nature had the power of sorrow, suffering, sacrifice, love and beauty in a subordinate state. Therefore, he encouraged women to realize these aspects of their religious nature as well as their general nature of subordination.

Because Bushnell placed such a high value on women's religious nature, he wished to entrust the task of building a strong foundation for the church to women, rather than to men. By making use of female religious nature, he hoped to form a solid church—an important institution for the creation of a Christian America.

In addition, Bushnell believed that it would not be women's political power, but their religious nature that would transform America into God's empire. This transformation would be accomplished through women's religious contributions in the church.

Bushnell was actually much more open to women's roles in the church than has been previously thought—provided men's government of women and women's subordination to men were retained. For instance, he supported women as public preachers. He also regarded the role of the deaconess as crucial, and believed that the deaconess was engaged in "common ministry" with pastors. In addition, he viewed the role of the minister's wife as significant and he thought that her involvement in Christian ministry was one of the effective ways to religiously transform the nation into a Christian America.

Despite his openness to female ministry, Bushnell did reject women's administration in the church. He thought that women taking on governing functions in the church would threaten the patriarchal and hierarchical order of men and women in the church. Thus, it is clear that he also had complex views of women's roles in the church.

Bushnell was a consistent anti-suffragist throughout his life. He saw the women's suffrage movement as a serious crisis in the history of the American nation—a crisis equal to the one that occurred during the period of the Revolutionary fathers. In his opinion, the women's suffrage movement was ideologically related to the idea of natural rights and the social compact theory of government, both of which were crucially important concepts of the Revolutionary fathers—particularly Thomas Jefferson. It was because women's suffrage aligned itself with these two theories that Bushnell ideologically opposed the movement. He held an unshakeable opinion that natural rights and the social compact theory would threaten a Christian America based on the organic unity of family, church, and nation.

Bushnell feared that if the women's suffrage movement was successful, the results would have a devastating impact on the family. For instance, he thought that, once women had the right to vote, they would want neither marriage nor children, that they would be inclined to divorce, and that they would no longer be interested in nurturing children. In short, he was afraid that the family would be destroyed by the women's suffrage movement.

In addition, Bushnell worried that the women's suffrage movement would disturb the Christianization of America through the church—something for which male ministers had labored for a century. In other words, he was fearful that a numerical decline of Christians would occur because Christian wives (who once encouraged their husbands and children to become members of the church) would shift their interests to political matters, such as women's suffrage. Thus, he clearly feared that the women's suffrage movement would weaken the foundation of the church, as well as the foundations of family and nation, and would thereby threaten a Christian America based on the organic unity of family, church, and nation.

When Bushnell envisioned a Christian America, women were totally excluded from the political arena. He thoroughly rejected their participation in politics through his opposition to women's suffrage. This is a crucial characteristic of his plan for building a Christian America. However, apart from female suffrage, he did allow women a number of important roles that he believed would support the growth of a Christian America. He encouraged females to increase the nation's population through marriage and childbirth, and to see that they nurtured their children in Christian values and principles. Moreover, he expected women to add their support by preaching and being deaconesses in the church. Furthermore, he encouraged women to uphold a Christianized America by entering various professions, such as teaching, medicine, law, art, writing, and business as well as by going into other arenas such as almshouses, hospitals, and common schools.

Therefore, except for the political field, Bushnell believed the women's sphere could be much more expanded in society. Also, from his perspective, there was not necessarily a sharp separation between the spheres of women and men. Rather, he believed that the spheres of women and men ought to overlap in society. Although scholars have previously believed that Bushnell limited women's sphere to the home, it is clear that he did not object to women's participation in broader activities in church and society, as long as the activities did not include the political arena or other types of governance. Thus, Bushnell had complex views of women in the political world and the other areas of society.

In summary, Bushnell's views on women were complex in terms of building a Christian America based on the organic unity of family, church, and nation. On the one hand, his views of women were patriarchal and hierarchical, emphasizing the different natures of men and women in such areas as the ideal family life, women's administration in church, and women's participation in the political world. On the other hand, his views on women were egalitarian and nurturing with regard to his actual family life, women's preaching and deaconesses' work in church, and women's access to various professions in society.

Contribution and Significance of This Book to Bushnell Scholarship

Although scholars have investigated Bushnell from various perspectives, his views on women's issues have been generally neglected. In particular, his views on women's issues in terms of a Christian America based on the organic unity of family, church, and nation have been completely ignored. In light of the emphasis on women's issues during the last two decades, this has left Bushnell scholarship with a significant void. I believe that the conclusions drawn from this study helped fill that void.

With regard to women's issues, especially women's suffrage, Bushnell spoke out against the historical tide. Because he was not in favor of women's suffrage, this seems to have been an unattractive field of study. However, excluding the negative aspects of a subject will present only one facet of history. In order for historical studies to be rich, both positive and negative aspects of a field of inquiry must be researched and critiqued. In this sense, I believe that even now, Bushnell is a significant and intriguing figure as an object of historical study regarding women's issues.

For Future Research

Finally, as a result of this study, the following issue has emerged for future research. It is obvious that Bushnell's views on women were a reaction to the social, cultural, historical, political and religious tide of his age. However, he seldom quoted from particular persons regarding women's issues. In addition, he was not an activist.[1] Therefore, it is difficult to identify precisely who influenced Bushnell regarding women's issues and whom Bushnell's ideas later influenced in history. In the future, research needs to be done in order to place Horace Bushnell within the history of people connected by their views of women's issues.

Notes

1 On this matter, refer to David Alan Jones' comment in "Christian America" in Chapter 4.

BIBLIOGRAPHY

Primary Sources

Bushnell, Horace. "The Age of Homespun." In *Work and Play*. New York: Charles Scribner, 1864.

________. "American Politics." *The American National Preacher* 14 (December 1840): 189-204.

________. *Barbarism the First Danger*. New York: The American Home Missionary Society, 1847.

________. *The Character of Jesus: Forbidding his Possible Classification with Men*. New York: Charles Scribner, 1861.

________. *Christian Nurture*. New York: Charles Scribner, 1861. Reprint, Grand Rapids: Baker Book House, 1979.

________. *Commemorative Discourse*. Hartford: Elihu Geer, 1853.

________. "Common Schools." In *Building Eras in Religion*, ed. Mary A. Bushnell, 71-105. New York: Charles Scribner's Sons, 1881.

Bushnell, Horace. *Crisis of the Church*. Hartford: Daniel Burgess and Co., 1835.

________. "The Doctrine of Loyalty." In *Work and Play*. New York: Charles Scribner, 1864.

________. *The Fathers of New England*. New York: Geo. P. Putnam, 1850.

________. *Forgiveness and Law, Grounded in Principles*. New York: Scribner, Armstrong & Co., 1874.

________. "God's Way with a Soul." In *Life and Letters of Horace Bushnell*, ed. Mary Bushnell Cheney, 1-2. New York: Harper & Brothers, Publishers, 1880. Reprint, New York: Arno Press & *The New York Times*, 1969.

________. "The Insight of Love." In *Christ and His Salvation: In Sermons Variously Related Thereto*. New York: Charles Scribner, 1864.

________. "A Marriage Ceremony." In *The Spirit in Man*, ed. Mary Bushnell Cheney, 385-87. New York: Charles Scribner's Sons, 1903.

________. "Mary, the Mother of Jesus." In *Sermons on Living Subjects*. New York: Charles Scribner's Sons, 1872.

________. *Moral Uses of Dark Things*. New York: Charles Scribner & Co., 1868.

________. *Nature and the Supernatural, as together Constituting the One System of God*. New York: Charles Scribner, 1858.

________. *Popular Government by Divine Right*. Hartford: L.E. Hunt, 1864.

________. *Reverses Needed*. Hartford: L.E. Hunt, 1861.

Bushnell, Horace. "Sketches of His Grandmother and Mother." In *Life and Letters of Horace Bushnell*, ed. Mary Bushnell Cheney, 24-34. New York: Harper & Brothers, Publishers, 1880. Reprint, Arno Press & *The New York Times*, 1969.

________. "The True Wealth or Weal of Nations." In *Work and Play*. New York: Charles Scribner, 1864.

________. *The Vicarious Sacrifice, Grounded in Principles of Universal Obligation*. New York: Charles Scribner & Co., 1866.

________. *Women's Suffrage; The Reform Against Nature*. New York: Charles Scribner and Company, 1869.

Cheney, Mary Bushnell, ed. *Life and Letters of Horace Bushnell*. New York: Harper & Brothers, Publishers, 1880. Reprint, New York: Arno Press & *The New York Times*, 1969.

Smith, David L., ed. *Horace Bushnell: Selected Writings on Language, Religion, and American Culture*. Chico: Scholars Press, 1984.

Secondary Sources

Anderson, Benedict. *Imagined Communities: Reflections on the Origin and Spread of Nationalism*. New York: Verso, 1991.

Baker, Paula. "The Domestication of Politics: Women and American Political Society, 1780-1920." *American Historical Review* 89 (1984): 620-47.

Banks, Oliver. *Faces of Feminism: A Study of Feminism as a Social Movement*. Cambridge: Basil Blackwell, 1981.

Barnes, Howard A. *Horace Bushnell and the Virtuous Republic*. Metuchen: The Scarecrow Press, Inc., 1991.

Barnes, Howard A. "The Idea That Caused a War: Horace Bushnell Versus Thomas Jefferson." *Journal of Church and State* 16, no. 1 (Winter 1974): 73-83.

Berderman, Gail. *Manliness & Civilization: A Cultural History of Gender and Race in the United States, 1880-1917.* Chicago: The University of Chicago Press, 1995.

Boyd, Lois A. "Presbyterian Ministers' Wives: A Nineteenth-Century Portrait." *Journal of Presbyterian History* 59 (1981): 3-17.

Braude, Ann. "Women's History Is American Religious History." In *Retelling U.S. Religious History*, ed. Thomas A. Tweed, 87-107. Berkeley: University of California Press, 1997.

Brownson, Orestes A. "The Woman Question, Article II." In *The Works of Orestes A. Brownson*, vol. XVIII, ed. Henry F. Brownson, 398-417. New York: AMS Press, Inc., 1966.

Buechler, Steven M. *Women's Movement in the United States: Woman Suffrage, Equal Rights, and Beyond.* New Brunswick and London: Rutgers University Press, 1990.

Cazden, Elizabeth. *Antoinette Brown Blackwell: A Biography.* New York: The Feminist Press, 1983.

Cherry, Conrad. *Nature and the Religious Imagination: From Edwards to Bushnell.* Philadelphia: Fortress, 1980.

________. "The Structure of Organic Thinking: Horace Bushnell's Approach to Language, Nature, and Nation." *Journal of the American Academy of Religion* 40 (1972): 3-20.

Clark, Jr., Clifford E. *Henry Ward Beecher: Spokesman for a Middle-Class American.* Chicago: University of Illinois Press, 1978.

Clinton, Catherine. *The Other Civil War: American Women in the Nineteenth Century.* New York: Hill and Wang, 1984.

Collens, Clarence Lyman. *Collins Memorial.* NP: Clarence Lyman Collens, 1959.

Cott, Nancy F. *The Bond of Womanhood: "Woman's Sphere" in the New England, 1780-1835.* New Haven and London: Yale University Press, 1977.

Cott, Nancy F. "On Men's History and Women's History." In *Meanings for Manhood: Construction of Masculinity in Victorian America*, ed. Mark C. Carnes and Clyde Griffen, 205-11. Chicago and London: The University of Chicago Press, 1990.

________. "Preface to the Second Edition: Then and Since." In *The Bonds of Womanhood: "Woman's Sphere" in New England, 1780-1835*. New Haven and London: Yale University Press, 1997.

________, et al. "Beyond Roles, Beyond Spheres: Thinking about Gender in the Early Republic." *William and Mary Quarterly* 46 (July 1989): 565-85.

Coudert, Allison. "Angels." In *The Encyclopedia of Religion*. vol. 1. 1987.

Cross, Barbara M. *Horace Bushnell: Minister to a Changing America*. Chicago: The University of Chicago Press, 1958.

Davies, Horton. "Congregationalist." In *A New Dictionary of Liturgy & Worship*. 1986.

Dayton, Donald W. *Discovering An Evangelical Heritage*. Peabody: Hendrickson Publishers, Inc., 1976.

Degler, Carl N. *At Odds: Women and the Family in America from the Revolution to the Present*. New York: Oxford University Press, 1980.

Douglas, Ann. *The Feminization of American Culture*. New York: Doubleday, 1977.

DuBois, Ellen Carol. *Feminism and Suffrage: The Emergence of an Independent Women's Movement in America, 1848-1869*. Ithaca and London: Cornell University Press, 1978.

Duke, James O. *Horace Bushnell: On the Vitality of Biblical Language*. Chico: Scholars Press, 1984.

"Editors' Table." *Godey's Lady's Book and Magazine* 491 (May 1871): 476.

Edwards, Mark. "'My God and My Good Mother': The Irony of Horace Bushnell's Gendered Republic." *Religion and American Culture: A Journal of Interpretation* 13, no. 1 (2003): 111-37.

Edwards, Robert L. *Of Singular Genius, Of Singular Grace: A Biography of Horace Bushnell.* Cleveland: The Pilgrim Press, 1992.

________. "Portrait of a People: Horace Bushnell's Hartford Congregation." In *Studies of the Church in History*, ed. Horton Davies, 149-63. Allison Park: Pickwick Publications, 1983.

________. *The Prow of the Ship: Preachers and Preaching over 150 Years*. Hartford: The Bond Press Incorporated, 1979.

Frothingham, O. B. "Is There Such a Thing as Sex?." *The Nation* 8 (January-June 1869): 87-89.

Gaventa, Beverly Roberts. "Romans." In *The Women's Bible Commentary*. 1992.

Guelzo, Allen C. "Foreword." In *The Puritan as Yankee: A Life of Horace Bushnell.* Grand Rapids: William B. Eerdmans Publishing Company, 2002.

Hackett, David G. "Gender and Religion in American Culture, 1870-1930." *Religion and American Culture* 5, no. 2 (Summer 1995): 127-57.

Halttunen, Karen. *Confidence Men and Painted Women: A Study of Middle-Class Culture in America, 1830-1870.* New Haven: Yale University Press, 1982.

Hambrick-Stowe, Charles E. *Charles G. Finney and the Spirit of American Evangelicalism*. Grand Rapids: William B. Eerdmans Publishing Company, 1996.

Handy, Robert T. *A Christian America: Protestant Hopes and Historical Realities*. New York: Oxford University Press, 1984.

________. "Sunday School Movement." In *The Westminster Dictionary of Christian Education*. 1963.

Hogeland, Ronald William. "Femininity and the Nineteenth Century Post-Puritan Mind." Ph.D. diss., University of California, Los Angeles, 1968.

Howe, Daniel Walker. *Making the American Self: Jonathan Edwards to Abraham Lincoln*. Cambridge: Harvard University Press, 1997.

________. *The Political Culture of the American Whigs*. Chicago and London: The University of Chicago Press, 1979.

________. "The Social Science of Horace Bushnell." *The Journal of American History* 70, no. 2 (September 1983): 305-22.

Hudson, Winthrop S., and John Corrigan. *Religion in America,* 5th ed. New York: Macmillan Publishing Company, 1992.

James, William. "Bushnell's Women's Suffrage." *The North American Review* 109 (October 1869): 556-65.

Jeffrey, Julie Roy. "Ministry Through Marriage: Methodist Clergy Wives on the Trans-Mississippi Frontier." In *Women in New Worlds: Historical Perspectives on the Wesleyan Tradition*, vol. 1, ed. Hilah F. Thomas and Rosemary Skinner Keller, 143-60. Nashville: Abingdon, 1981.

Jones, David Alan. "The Social and Political Thought of Horace Bushnell: An Interpretation of the Mid-Nineteenth-Century American Mind." Ph.D. diss., Northwestern University, Evanston, 1973.

Kent, John. "The Character and Possibility of Christian Theology Today." In *Companion Encyclopedia of Theology*. 1995.

Kerber, Linda K. "Separate Spheres, Female Worlds, Woman's Place: The Rhetoric of Women's History." *The Journal of American History* 75, no. 1 (June 1988): 9-39.

Kimmel, Michel. *Manhood in America: A Cultural History*. New York: The Free Press, 1996.

Lawler, Michael G. "Sacrament of Marriage." In *The New Dictionary of Sacramental Worship*. 1990.

Lerner, Gerda. *The Creation of Patriarchy*. New York: Oxford University Press, 1986.

Lindley, Susan Hill. *"You Have Stept Out Of Your Place": A History of Women and Religion in America*. Louisville: Westminster John Knox Press, 1996.

Little, Sara. "Christian Nurture." *American Presbyterians* 66 (Winter 1988): 245-50.

Marshall, Susan E. *Splintered Sisterhood: Gender and Class in the Campaign against Woman Suffrage*. Madison: The University of Wisconsin Press, 1997.

McCant, Jerry W. "Nurture Is Not the Problem." *Christian Education Journal* 5, no. 2 (1984): 57-68.

McDannell, Colleen. *The Christian Home in Victorian America, 1840-1900*. Bloomington: Indiana University Press, 1986.

Miller, Randolph Crump. *Christian Nurture and the Church*. New York: Charles Scribner's Sons, 1961.

________. "Horace Bushnell: Prophet to America's Children." *Perkins Journal* 32 (1979): 1-8.

Moorhead, James H. *American Apocalypse: Yankee Protestants and the Civil War, 1860-1869*. New Haven and London: Yale University Press, 1978.

Mulder, John M. "Introduction." In *Christian Nurture*, by Horace Bushnell. Reprint, Grand Rapids: Baker Book House, 1979.

Mullin, Robert Bruce. *The Puritan as Yankee: A Life of Horace Bushnell*. Grand Rapids: William B. Eerdmans Publishing Company, 2002.

Nichols, Carole. *Votes and More for Women: Suffrage and After in Connecticut*. New York: The Institute for Research in History and The Haworth Press, Inc., 1983.

Olbricht, T. H. "Prayer Meeting." In *Dictionary of Christianity in America*. 1990.

Olson, Jeannine E. *One Ministry[,] Many Roles: Deacons and Deaconesses through the Centuries*. St. Louis: Concordia Publishing House, 1992.

Reynolds, Davis S. "The Feminization Controversy: Sexual Stereotypes and the Paradoxes of Piety in Nineteenth-Century America." *The New England Quarterly* 53 (1980): 96-106.

Rotundo, E. Anthony. *American Manhood: Transformations in Masculinity from the Revolution to the Modern Era*. New York: BasicBooks, 1993.

Rugoff, Milton. *The Beechers: An American Family in the Nineteenth Century*. New York: Harper & Row, Publishers, 1981.

Ryan, Halford R. *Henry Ward Beecher: Peripatetic Preacher*. New York: Greenwood Press, 1990.

Ryan, Mary P. *The Empire of the Mother: American Writing about Domesticity, 1830-1860*. New York: The Institute for Research in History and The Haworth Press, 1982.

Schuyler, David. "Inventing a Feminine Past." *The New England Qvarterly*, 51 (September 1978): 291-308.

Shiels, Richard D. "The Feminization of American Congregationalism, 1730-1835." *American Quarterly* 39 (1981): 46-62.

Sklar, Kathryn Kish. *Catharine Beecher: A Study in American Domesticity*. New York: W.W. Norton & Company, Inc., 1976.

Smith, David L. *Symbolism and Growth: The Religious Thought of Horace Bushnell*. Chico: Scholars Press, 1981.

Smith, J. Eugene. *One Hundred Years of Hartford's Courant: From Colonial Times through the Civil War*. New Haven: Yale University Press, 1949.

Stanton, Elizabeth Cady et al. *The Woman's Bible: Part I, Comments on Genesis, Exodus, Leviticus, Numbers and Deuteronomy.* New York: European Publishing Company, 1895.

________, et al. *The Woman's Bible: Part II, Comments on the Old and New Testaments from Joshua to Revelation.* New York: European Publishing Company, 1898.

Stanton, Elizabeth Cady; Anthony, Susan B.; and Gage, Matilda Joslyn, eds. *History of Woman Suffrage.* Vol. I. Rochester: Charles Mann, 1887.

________. *History of Woman Suffrage.* Vol. III. Rochester: Charles Mann, 1887.

Sweet, Leonard I. *The Minister's Wife: Her Role in Nineteenth-Century American Evangelicalism.* Philadelphia: Temple University Press, 1983.

Taves, Ann. "Mother and Children and the Legacy of Mid-nineteenth-Century American Christianity." *Journal of Religion* 67, no. 2 (1987): 203-19.

Watson, Harry L. *Liberty and Power: The Politics of Jacksonian America.* New York: Hill and Wang, 1989.

Weaver, Glenn. *Hartford: An Illustrated History of Connecticut's Capital.* Woodland: Windsor Publications, Inc., 1982.

Weld, Stanley B. *The History of Immanuel Church, 1824-1967.* Hartford: Connecticut Printers, Incorporated, 1968.

Welter, Barbara. "The Cult of True Womanhood: 1800-1860." In *Dimity Convictions: The American Woman in the Nineteenth Century.* Athens: Ohio University Press, 1976.

________. "The Feminization of American Religion: 1800-1860." In *Dimity Convictions: The American Woman in the Nineteenth Century.* Athens: Ohio University Press, 1976.

Welter, Barbara. "Something Remains to Dare: Introduction to *The Woman's Bible*." In *The Original Feminist Attack on the Bible*, by Elizabeth Cady Stanton. Reprint, New York: Arno Press, 1974.

White, Charles Edward. *The Beauty of Holiness: Phoebe Palmer as Theologian, Revivalist, Feminist, and Humanitarian*. Grand Rapids: Francis Asbury Press, 1986.

Why, Joseph S. "Crusaders of the Pen and Podium: Henry Ward Beecher, Thomas K. Beecher and Other Family Members." In *Portraits of a Nineteenth Century Family: A Symposium on the Beecher Family*, ed. Earl A. French and Diana Royce, 99-127. Hartford: The Stowe-Day Foundation, 1976.

Youngs, J. William T. *The Congregationalists*. New York: Greenwood Press, 1990.

Zikmund, Barbara Brown. "The Struggle for the Right to Preach." In *Women and Religion in America: The Nineteenth Century*, ed. Rosemary Radford Ruether and Rosemary Skinner Keller, 193-205. San Francisco: Harper & Row, Publishers, 1981.

INDEX

ABOUT THE AUTHOR

Michiyo Morita is Associate Professor at the General Research Institute, Seigakuin University (Ageo, Japan). She received a B.A. in Education from Saga National University (Saga, Japan), an M.Edu. in Philosophy of Education from International Christian University (Tokyo, Japan), an M.T.S. with *summa cum laude* from Drew University (Madison, New Jersey), and a Ph.D. in American Religion and Culture, also from Drew University. A Horace Bushnell scholar, she has written articles in Japanese, "Development from *Discourses on Christian Nurture* through *Christian Nurture* by Horace Bushnell" for *The Japan Journal of Christian Education*, and "A Christian America Horace Bushnell Envisioned" for *The Journal of Campus Ministry*, in addition to "A Controversy on *Christian Nurture* between Bennet Tyler and Horace Bushnell" and "Horace Bushnell's View on Women's Suffrage" for *The Journal of General Research Institute at Seigakuin University*. Her Japanese translation of Bushnell's *Christian Nurture (Part I)* will be published in 2004 by Seigakuin University Press.